DALES LAW

Dales Law

A Country Solicitor's Year

John Francis

First published in 1991 by
Smith Settle Ltd
Ilkley Road
Otley
West Yorkshire
LS21 3JP

Reprinted 1992

ISBN Paperback 1 870071 80 8
Hardback 1 870071 81 6

Designed, printed and bound by
SMITH SETTLE
Ilkley Road, Otley, West Yorkshire LS21 3JP

Dedication

I dedicate this book to my wife Rosemary,
without whose love, encouragement and support
it would not have been written, and who shares
with me a deep appreciation of all manner
of country things and a particular affection
for the Yorkshire Dales and for the warmth and humour
of its people.

Acknowledgements

I take this opportunity of gratefully acknowledging the help and advice I have received from many people in the course of writing this book, not least from my own family, and my partners, staff and clients.

I wish particularly to thank Mrs Lucile Bell for permitting me to quote from her late husband Mr John Moore's book *English Comedy*. I am indebted to Mr Patrick Harvey for allowing me to quote from the poems of his late father, F W Harvey. The family of the late Alexander Pearson have kindly given permission to quote from his book *Doings of a Country Solicitor*.

Permission to quote from *Murder in the Cathedral* by T S Eliot and from *Poem XXX (To Christopher Isherwood)* by W H Auden has been granted by Faber & Faber Ltd; and the quotations from the poems of Hilaire Belloc are reprinted by the kind permission of the Peters Fraser & Dunlop Group Ltd.

I have also quoted various lawyers, poets, writers, naturalists and sportsmen who may be beyond the reach of copyright but are certainly not beyond the courtesy of an acknowledgement. I am most grateful to them all.

Author's Note

This book describes a year in my life as a country solicitor, but it is a typical year rather than any particular year. There are references to real Yorkshire place names, but the reader will not be able to find Denley on any map, for it is an amalgam of the different towns and villages in which I have practised over the years. Most of the people described are composites or wholly imaginary too, but will be familiar to many practising solicitors as 'character types'.

Contents

Chapter One

'The sedge is withered from the lake
And no birds sing'
    John Keats

It takes a poet to sum up winter in just one sentence, but 'Owd Jacob', lifelong countryman, one-time farm labourer, and friend and guide throughout my Yorkshire boyhood, had some more practical words to offer when Rosemary and I were about to face the first Dales winter of our married life.

'Tha wants a sack o' flour an' sum yist', he counselled her, knowing that she baked her own bread.

She was glad she had taken his advice a few weeks later when we were snowed in by huge drifts.

It has not been too bad so far this year. I have benefited from the few days after Christmas when the office was quiet, and cleared up most of the backlog of work which I had abandoned when I went off with my partners and staff to the office Christmas party before the holidays.

A solicitor's job is not a seasonal one in the same way that it is for hoteliers, farmers or cricketers, but if there is ever a quiet time to be had in the office it is generally the New Year.

This is certainly true at Boothroyd and Lytton, the old-established firm of family solicitors in the Dales market town of Denley where I have worked for the past thirty years, starting as a very raw articled clerk and progressing to my present position of senior partner. Not that I have any delusions of grandeur in holding this title, for all it really means is that I am getting older!

There are, it is true, a few drink-driving cases at this time of year, and the inevitable matrimonial cases arising curiously and rather sadly from the fact that some husbands and wives have spent too much time in each other's company over the holidays! Apart from these, it is generally quiet, too soon after Christmas for people to be buying and selling houses, and too early for clients to succumb to the effects of winter and provide us with probate work.

In a solicitor's office, however, you always have to be ready for the unexpected. My quiet catching-up was disturbed by my secretary Clare, who interrupted me to say that there was a highly agitated man in reception.

Ned Sellars is a smallholder who makes his living by mending and servicing local farmers' tractors, wagons and other agricultural machinery. He stood in the doorway of my office, looking decidedly scruffy in his dirty corduroys and torn sports jacket, and as he moved towards me in his muddy boots, he raised his greasy hands in the air and looked absolutely livid as he exclaimed:

'There's nowt for it, Mr Francis, Ah've med me mind up an' Ah'll not go back on t' job. Yon bugger's got it comin' to 'im an' Ah'm not reet fussed whether 'e's suited. 'E needs tekkin' tae court – an' that's wheer tha comes in, Mr Francis.'

He paused for a moment to catch breath in the midst of this indignant flow.

'Would you please come in, Mr Sellars, and take a seat. Can you start again from the beginning so that I've got a straight tale. Then I'll be able to advise you properly.'

Ned still waxed indignant and carried on as if I had not spoken.

'That bugger Jim Braithwaite – tha knows 'im, that bloody stuck-up farmer ovver Grassdale way – well Ah fettled up 'is tractor reet enough but t' bugger won't pay. An' Ah reckons, now it's t' turn o' t' year, like, that 'e's gitten to be med to pay.'

Ned temporarily ran out of breath.

'You're telling me that a farmer called Jim Braithwaite owes you money for repairing his tractor. How much was your bill?'

'It were a fifty pund job but it's not t' brass, like, it's t' principle', replied Ned.

'When was the work done and the debt incurred?'

Ned scratched his head and thought for a minute before replying.

'Ah were reckoning it up t' other day, it were seventeen year ago as last Tuesday.'

'Seventeen years ago?', I exclaimed. 'Have you ever heard of the Statute of Limitations?'

I had asked the question of a lawyer instinctively. It was an ill-judged question to put to a Yorkshire farmer, as I immediately realised from Ned's blank look.

'You can't sue on a debt that's more than six years old', I explained to him.

'Yer mean yon bugger's goin' to git away wi'out payin'?', Ned asked indignantly.

'It means, Mr Sellars, that you've allowed him to get away without paying for too long. You've left it too late.'

Ned got up and walked slowly to the door, shaking his head in disbelief.

'Nay', he said, 'its not reet, all them years an' Ah did nowt about t' job.'

He stood silently for a minute before firing his parting shot:

'An' Ah suppose tha'll want paying an' all?'

People like Ned never like being told what they don't want to hear, I reflected, still less do they like paying for such advice. Ned's New Year resolution to recover a seventeen year old debt had just been tried – and found wanting.

One of my own New Year resolutions was not to attend any of the whist drives advertised at this time of year in the local press. Having been brought up in a village, I already knew all about those two money-raising pillars of village life, jumble sales and whist drives. I knew very well that jumble sales could be quite good fun – that is after you had recovered from the shock of seeing the Charge of the Light Brigade re-enacted, and you had come to terms with the sight of otherwise highly respectable women throwing all niceties of behaviour to the wind and being caught up in the sort of mob hysteria which afflicts young girls when they catch sight of their favourite pop star.

Jumble sales were alright, I reckoned, but whist drives were to be avoided at all costs – and for good reason. When I attended my first village whist drive, I made the cardinal mistake of failing to realise just how seriously whist players take their game. I had learnt the basics from my Scottish granny: 'Remember dear, second player plays low, and always follow suit'.

In the very first game of the evening I found myself partnering Bert Snowball, a retired farmer who made it clear from the start that he was playing not for fun but to win.

'Na then, lad, Ah'm countin' on thee', he said without a glimmer of a smile.

In the concluding and decisive rubber I allowed my concentration to lapse. I just could not allow myself to be serious about a game like whist. After all, card games are not like cricket, I thought. I was quickly and violently brought back to earth by Bert, who banged his large and horny fist on the table. He spoke just two words:

'Nay, lad.'

The tone of his voice was a mixture of anger, contempt and disbelief. As I met his icy stare and looked at the cards on the table, I realised the magnitude of my crime. I had just trumped his winning card. There was a long silence, much head shaking and tut-tutting before my partner spoke again.

'An' thee an educated man!', exclaimed Bert.

That is why, every New Year from that calamitous evening onwards, I have resolved never to play in a village whist drive again.

In January I don't want to go to whist drives – in fact I don't want to do anything very much. Like the trees and plants in my garden, I just want to take a rest, put my feet up with a good book in front of a log fire and only come to life with the sunshine, flowers and butterflies of early spring.

Like the office, the dale, too, is quiet. Quiet, that is, in its still fields and leafless trees, but even now there are still too many cars and tourists. The days are gone when in the winter months the locals had the dale to themselves. The consolation is that even though on the first decent Sunday, Denley can be full of visitors, very few stray more than fifty yards from where they have parked their cars. So many people come to the countryside, but so few people really see it, understand it or appreciate it. Even on Bank Holidays, Rosemary and I have walked on the moors and not met a living soul, whilst only a mile away in the town the streets and the shops will be full of people and noise and bustle.

During a cold snap we have had problems with mice getting into the house, notwithstanding the presence of our cat Lily. Now although Rosemary and I are both really dog people, we have always had cats right from the early days of our married life, when we were 'adopted' by a stray tabby which very shortly afterwards gave birth to a litter of kittens.

Lily is a strange cat, shy, nervous and spending a lot of time off on her own, but if Rosemary and I cannot quite reckon her up, our daughter Melanie, who is apparently on her same spiritual wavelength, understands her, loves her and spoils her shamelessly.

14

For this reason Lily is not much help to us in solving the mice problem, so I have to do what I had to do frequently as a boy, namely to catch them in those fiendish but deadly 'Little Nipper' mousetraps. Quicker and less painful than being played with and tormented by a cat, but absolutely lethal. As a schoolboy, I spent quite a lot of time dealing with mice one way or another because, apart from being the family's resident 'rodent control operative', I was also the proud keeper of pet mice, firstly inside the house and later, when my family could put up with the smell no longer, outside in the woodshed.

I feel rather squeamish at the prospect of killing mice now; how cissy me as a boy would have thought me now, but then boys tend not to think very deeply or sensitively about these matters. Certainly it never struck me as at all odd or contradictory as a boy that, on the one hand I should be a member of the National Mouse Club and spend hours teaching my pet mice to jump through hoops and do other tricks in their cages, and on the other hand that I should be a past master at setting mouse traps and held what must surely have been the village record for the number of mice caught and killed by that method. Even as a boy, I was sorry when the victim in the trap was a long-tailed fieldmouse with its whiskery face, donkey ears and eyes which looked at me in surprise.

Lily is too well fed – the mice are multiplying. I must harden my heart and set some more traps.

January is my least favourite month. I don't care much for winter walking, except when I'm out on the moors beagling, it is too wet to do much in the garden, the days are dark and cheerless, and there are no butterflies except for a solitary peacock which I found hibernating in the outbuilding.

The peacock is surely one of the most handsome of butterflies. Its black underside with a steely sheen crossed by irregular black lines belies its multicoloured upperside, the highlights of which are are the 'peacock eyes'. A specimen was recorded in 1900 flying over the snow in February, but the butterfly generally stays in hibernation until the spring. It is, however, more often than not seen in late summer and autumn, and I shall always associate it with the garden flowers of that season, especially buddleia, phlox and sedum.

Even in this dreary month, nature still provides us with consolation. The snowdrops, crocuses and daffodils are starting to make headway, the days are slowly but surely starting to lengthen, and on the first decent day I can begin thinking about the start of the tennis season and to seeing the first butterfly on the wing.

Back at the office, things are starting to return to normal after Christmas and New Year. I certainly felt my own practice was getting back to normal when, after a few days of routine work, I received a visit from James Bottomley, one of my oldest and most persistent clients.

Whenever in the past he came to the office – which was often – it was always to complain, generally about his neighbours or his health, but if it was neither of these then it would be about something he had bought, someone who had offended him or about one of the frequent misfortunes he had suffered. He was by now over seventy years old, his frame was bent beneath a dirty old raincoat, and his dismal dress and appearance were perfectly set off by the perpetual hang-dog expression on his face. Although he was a well-known local character, nobody had ever discovered what he actually did for a living, but it was widely believed that he had a considerable private fortune.

At first we all knew him in the office as 'String of Misery', but I later gave him the new nickname of 'Lucky Jim' when I realised that the first word he always uttered when he came into my office was '*Un*fortunately', a word he always spoke slowly, loudly and with a huge Yorkshire emphasis on the first syllable. This word was always the prelude to yet another tale of woe which went on interminably and in excruciating detail.

'Na wheer were Ah, Mr Francis? Aye well, as Ah were tellin' thee, me Land Rovver cut out on me ovver Dallowgill way. Theer Ah were, an' jus' me luck it were silin' down wi' rain, like. Ah say, t' job 'appened once afore when t' garage tell'd me there'd be no further bother wi' t' engine. Ah paid good money to 'em to fettle t'car up an' wheer dus it get yer, Mr Francis, Ah ask yer, jus' wheer dus it get yer? Well, *un*fortunately, there were no telephone up on yon moor an' Ah got soaked to t' skin afore Ah flagged down a young feller in a sports car. But when Ah gets into t' car an' sets off wi 'im, like, *un*fortunately he tells me 'e's not goin' to Denley wheer Ah wants to be, but 'es mekkin 'is way to bloody 'arrogate – an' thats wheer we landed. Ah says to 'im: "This is no good to me young feller, Ah needs to be back in Denley". An' d'yer know, Mr

Francis, 'e tells me to catch t' bus. They're all t' same these young uns. *Un*fortunately, t' bus were late an' Ah 'ad to wait jus' short of an hour an' ten minutes afore it came, an' Ah were another half hour when Ah gets back to Denley.'

I had by this time listened long enough and interrupted quickly.

'Are you asking me, Mr Bottomley, if you have any claim against the garage for not repairing your car properly? If so I suggest the first thing you do is to get an independent mechanic to give you a report, and then if you've got the evidence ask the garage to put the car right free of charge. If this fails, get the work done by another garage at the expense of the first garage.'

'Nay, Mr Francis, it's not that, Ah've already got t' car job sorted out. What Ah wants to know is whether Ah can get t' cost of me bus fare back from that cocky young bugger in t' sports car?'

After I had taken my leave of 'Lucky Jim', following what I considered to be a fairly succinct reply to his question, I turned to my secretary Clare, whose encyclopaedic knowledge of Denley and its people makes her an invaluable member of the firm.

'The holidays are well and truly over', I said. 'It's back to business as usual.'

Clare, seeing the exasperated expression on my face, nodded understandingly, for she knew 'Lucky Jim' of old and guessed accurately that I had just been compelled to listen to yet another tale of woe from this well-known local character.

'What was it this time, Mr Francis?', she asked, 'his health or his neighbours? Some people are their own worst enemies', she added philosophically.

It is not often realised, I think, just how much secretaries like Clare help solicitors to see their work in its proper perspective.

So far, apart from a short cold snap, it's been a green month, reminding me of the year when the children were younger and we bought them all toboggans for Christmas. As luck would have it, there was no snow that winter until early April, when the children, who had been champing at the bit to go sledging, were at last able to have a few runs down our field until the snow melted in the strengthening spring sunshine.

There doesn't seem to have been the snow and ice in recent winters that there used to be, but I suspect that folk in every generation have probably made this observation, or something like it.

17

Certainly when I was a boy there seemed to be snowfall every winter, and always at least one spell of frost which enabled us to skate on Ilkley tarn or Yeadon dam. The *Yorkshire Evening Post* carried reports of 'Skating Prospects' at such times, and if I was sufficiently encouraged by these reports, then off to the ice I and my friends would go. I used to screw my skates on the bottom of my football boots, and for an indifferent skater like myself the support to the ankles which those boots gave was absolutely invaluable. The light flimsy footwear which passes for football boots nowadays would have been quite useless. There would then follow an hour or two of skating, a shared thermos flask of hot tea by the edge of the tarn and then, as dusk fell, back home to a cosy evening by a log fire.

I think that one of the reasons we don't notice winter so much these days, even in the country, is the widespread availability of central heating – a very acceptable invention of modern times. I should not myself care to go back to the days when I could see my breath in the bedroom, and had to scrape the frost with my fingernails from the inside of the window.

I suppose that the worst winter in living memory was in 1947, which I can just remember as a small boy, a winter which was too cruel for the British people so tired after the war. I remember rather better the glorious summer which followed it, the great butterfly summer, not only for our own native species but also for migrants like the clouded yellows, which at nightfall littered the ground where they settled in thousands on the Isle of Anglesey where my family holidayed that memorable summer. I wonder whether I shall ever live to see another 'clouded yellow year' like that one?

The contrasting seasons of 1947 remind us that nature has a marvellous way of redressing imbalances, and countrymen particularly know that the cruellest winter can turn into the loveliest spring, and that the severest drought is surely followed by plenteous reservoir-filling rain. We should not worry too much about extremes of weather.

I often remind myself of an old Dalesman's comment one Sunday as we stood outside church, where we had just prayed for relief from a severe drought.

'Now think on, Mr Francis', he remarked as he cast his eyes heavenwards. 'There's a better provider than us, tha knows.'

There's always something new to learn every day in a solicitors's office; if you don't feel that, you are clearly past it. There is also – and this is the solicitor's salvation in the face of all the boring and repetitive work – something that is said or happens every day to make him laugh. It was a dismal day when old Ernie Bradley provided such a moment quite unintentionally.

'I never knew you were such a religious man, Mr Francis', he said to me, after I had advised him on a problem relating to his family business.

I looked at him puzzled for a moment. Then all became clear as he pointed to the Bible which lay on the table at the side of my desk.

'Oh', I said, 'the reason I keep a Bible there is because I'm a commissioner for oaths and I need to have one handy when people come in to be sworn to affidavits and so forth.'

'That's it, is it,' replied Ernie, 'and there was I thinking what a religious man you must be having a Bible at your side all the time.'

As old Ernie left the office, I couldn't help smiling to myself at the recollection of the time many years ago when I was actually appointed a commissioner for oaths by the Lord Chancellor, and I attempted to explain my duties to my young son. My efforts were unsuccessful – he couldn't for the young life of him understand why perfect strangers should walk in off the street into his father's office in order to swear at him.

'I'll just call you "a daddy of oaths"', he said finally.

Nowadays any qualified solicitor can act as a commissioner for oaths and young solicitors seem very adept at cornering this particular market, so I don't get as many oath fees as used to be the case. To my own and to earlier generations of solicitors, oath fees were always regarded as 'baccy money', but as I fill my pipe I have had to come to terms with the fact that even these payments are now subject to VAT. Is nothing sacred?

I don't usually do much gardening in winter, but there is at least one job I must do this time of year. My family gave me a greengage tree for Christmas and I must plant it. The poor man's plum, as it has always been known, is a fruit I shall always associate with childhood, for there was an old man in our village who grew a marvellous greengage tree at the bottom of his cottage garden, where he also kept pet rabbits in ramshackle, home-made hutches. This tree was a boy's delight in late summer when it was laden with fruit, and when my friends and I got tummy ache with eating too many of them, there were still baskets of fruit to bring home for making into delicious pies and puddings.

I decided to plant the tree in a corner of my garden near to two Victoria plum trees which, unexpectedly in our Northern climate and in their rather windy and exposed position, have fruited well every year. I remembered my gardening mentor 'Owd Jacob' once telling me that greengages need a Victoria plum tree somewhere handy to pollinate them. As I dug the hole, put in some well-rotted muck at the bottom and drove in the supporting stake, I could hear him saying to me:

'Gie it sum space lad, tease out t' toes a bit. Plant it reet an' it'll not tek any fault.'

Jacob always used the old Yorkshire 'toes' for roots, a dialect word so descriptive and so apt. I widened the hole to make sure the 'toes' of the tree were not cramped or doubled up, teased them out a bit, then put the soil back and firmed the tree in with my boots.

Planting a tree, I always think, is an act of faith in the future of mankind and of our planet. I can only hope that long after my garden has passed into others' hands, my small greengage tree will bring pleasure with its leafy shade and late summer bounty.

Of all the jobs in the office which get me down, dealing with local authorities comes pretty near the top of my list. Speaking to anyone at the council who is willing to make a decision or to accept responsibility for anything is virtually impossible, and if after telling your story to at least six different people you finally make contact with the right person, you are as likely as not to be told that the matter has to go before a committee or that some additional document or plan is necessary.

Occasionally, but only very occasionally, I am presented with an opportunity to laugh when dealing with a council.

One day this month, I was acting for a someone who was purchasing a small piece of land from his local council. On his behalf, I sent off the usual search to the same council to make sure there were no planning matters which adversely affected the property. I attached a copy of the plan which the council had prepared and sent to me along with the draft contract. A few days later I received a telephone call from a council official.

'This plan you've sent me, Mr Francis, it won't do, it won't do at all', he said.

'What exactly is wrong with it?', I asked.

'It just won't do. We can't identify the property from it, and there's not enough detail.'

I was already smiling to myself by this time, and decided to lead him on a bit further.

'I'm sorry to hear you say that', I said, 'You reckon the plan is a bit of an amateur effort?'

'Yes, it definitely won't do for the council', he replied rather pompously.

'I think I should tell you that the plan in front of you was supplied to me by the council in the first place', I said.

'What...er...er...why has the council prepared the plan?'

'You obviously don't know or haven't realised that the council owns the land which my client is buying and which is the subject of the search.'

There was another embarrassed silence before I went on.

'It's clearly a case of the left hand not knowing what the right hand is doing. I'll leave you to have a word with whoever prepared that plan, and if you're still not happy with it then perhaps you could suggest that your colleague has another go at it!'

Prior to the 'reform' of local government in 1974, such a conversation would never have taken place. Local government in those days was truly local, which had great advantages for solicitors, particularly when dealing with property transactions. If you had a query about roads, Fred was the chap to speak to; if there was a drainage problem, then Joe was the resident expert; and Ernest, who had worked at the council for as long as anyone could remember, seemed to know the history and usage of just about every house in the district.

Local government now is just an expensive, inefficient and impersonal bureaucracy. How appalling too, I have often thought, that the same local government 'reforms' should have destroyed traditional counties like Rutland and Westmorland, and should have attempted to meddle with the boundaries of Yorkshire and our traditional Ridings. A good job that we Tykes do not take too much notice of these changes, and that until recently we still recognised traditional boundaries when it came to eligibility to play for the County Cricket Club.

This year the dark wintry days have been enlivened by two occurrences. Early in the month, a bull escaped into the town from Denley market and did considerable damage in several shops before being eventually caught. One of the shops was a china shop, so it was quite literally a case of 'the bull in the china shop'.

Then right at the end of the month, a prisoner escaped from the local magistrates court. I witnessed this event, having happened to go down to court to speak to our assistant solicitor who was representing a client there. A young lad of eighteen broke free as he was being led into the dock, got out through the side door and made his escape into the street. Although a serious matter, it produced some chuckles from those of us who watched him make his escape, for this slim, fit young man, dressed in T-shirt, jeans and wearing trainers, was being hopelessly pursued by Jack Flasby, a rather overweight, middle-aged police constable in full uniform and wearing heavy boots. We spectators unanimously judged that Jack had no chance. It was in fact several weeks before our young friend was recaptured and brought back to court under heavy police escort.

January always seems such a long month, a hard one for the birds too, but the helping hand we give them by way of bread crusts, nuts and fat on the bird table in our garden is more than rewarded by the sight, colours and antics of the numerous tits, robins, finches, nuthatches and sparrows which feed there.

It is the last day of the month, and we have had a week of hard frosts. Ours is sheep country and, during spells of hard frosts, countrymen notice that sheep are silent. The poet Keats noticed it too:

'St Agnes Eve, Ah bitter chill it was!
The owl, for all his feather was a-cold
The hare limp'd trembling through the frozen grass
And silent was the flock in woolly fold.'

It is a the time of year when the weathercock on top of Denley church spire turns north, there is a snow wind coming and the spirit is low. All we can do is to batten down the hatches, look forward to the lengthening days of February, and remind ourselves of Shelley's famous line:

'If Winter comes, can Spring be far behind?'

Chapter Two

*'February, fill the dyke
With what thou dost like.'*
Thomas Tusser

On the whole I find weather and season rhymesters rather tedious, but Tusser's couplet is surely an apt one hereabouts when the snow starts melting up the dale. As the month proceeds and I look forward to the first time I return home from the office in daylight, I remember too the other saying of the month:

'As the day lengthens, the cold strengthens.'

In the mild winter of 1975 I saw my first small tortoiseshell butterfly on the 7th February, but that pleasure is normally reserved for the first sunny day in March. There are snowdrops flowering in my garden, but they must stay there as country folk have always thought it unlucky to bring them indoors. Not much else is in flower, apart from the red dead nettles in the weedier part of the garden. On the lane side up at the back of the house there are a few bits of gorse, reminding me of the saying 'when gorse is in blossom, kissing's in fashion' – which must be true when one realises that gorse is in flower more or less all the year round.

The birds are generally quiet, being intent only on looking for food, but the brief and rarely heard winter song of the robin is worth the waiting; and the developing song of the other garden birds on milder days remind me that spring is not far away. Indeed spring has already begun underground, as evidenced by the new molehills in our field. The birdsong which I always anticipate most keenly at this time of year is that of the yellowhammer, when he sings his 'little bit of bread and no cheese'. My heart starts to lift, too, when the rooks start building their nests, and I see the tiny and rare goldcrest in the woods and the first cheeky pied wagtail in the garden.

We cannot have snowdrops in the house, but what Rosemary and I love to gather and bring indoors every year at this time are large bunches of pussy willow and hazel tree catkins. The latter, which have hung dull and lifeless for months, turn suddenly to a delicate yellow, almost incandescent in the sunlight, and their presence finally convinces us that the cycle of new life has really begun.

Back at the office, I am grappling as usual with my 'gumboot practice' and trying to get my farming clients to put their affairs in order.

The motto of farming brothers Fred and Joe Westgate must surely be: 'Never do today what you can put off until tomorrow'. 'Twas ever thus with these two, and it was no different when they came to see me one dreary day this month.

I knew that I wasn't going to get very far from the moment Fred walked in and told me that Joe couldn't come because ' 'e'd 'ad to see a chap at t' market aboot sum Mashams'.

'Now Fred', I said, 'I want to know if you and Joe have come to any decision about the proposals for your farming business I made to you eighteen months ago, and about the new wills and partnership agreement you were going to make.'

'Nay, Mr Francis, it's nivver eighteen month sin', is it?', replied Fred, shaking his head in apparent disbelief.

'I've got the copy letter here – it's eighteen months to the day.'

'Is that reight?', asked Fred, looking even more puzzled .

'Yes', I retorted, 'it's right enough and I suggest, in your interests, some definite decisions need to be made now.'

Knowing Fred of old, I could have written the script for his next line.

'Well, Mr Francis, it's like this yer see', said Fred, scratching his head, 'ivver sin' me father died, Joe an' me 'as worked t' farm between t' pair on us, an' 'e'll 'ave to 'ave 'is say afore Ah can tell thee owt. Wiv nivver bin out o' 'arness yet, an' Ah don't reckon to be settin' off on that road now.'

I sighed, resigning myself to the inevitable, and wondered only whether I would ever get the opportunity to deliver a bill to the brothers, let alone ever receive payment for my services.

'When Ah've spoke wi Joe', he went on decisively, 'Ah'll 'appen mek an appointment for t' pair on us. It'll be reight, Mr Francis, it'll be reight.'

I showed Fred to the door with a frozen smile on my face. It only thawed after he had left, and I thought of the vast multitude of Inland Revenue inspectors, VAT officers, planners, and other officials who for years had received exactly the same treatment, and whose efforts had been continually thwarted by the same tactics when the two brothers did not want to do something. Their need to consult each other about everything and on all occasions was their way of playing for time – and highly effective it was too.

'One of these days, I'll catch those two together', I said to my secretary Clare as I got down to working on the pile of files on my desk.

'That'll be the day', she replied knowingly.

The day after Fred's visit to my office, I went out of the office to see a new client. Solicitors are always anxious to make a favourable impression in such cases, and it was with this thought foremost in my mind that I set off to visit a widow called Isobel Franklin, who lived in a bungalow not far from Denley. My desire to please her was particularly strong, as she had been personally recommended to me.

It was a typical February day – not only was it cold and raw but it was raining as well. So when Mrs Franklin opened the front door to allow me inside, I left the door open for a short time to wipe my feet on the doormat. As I did so, a rather dirty looking sheepdog slipped past me, went through the hall and straight into the lounge. I followed Mrs Franklin and the dog into this room, which was undoubtedly one of the most beautifully furnished and immaculately tidy rooms I had ever seen in my life.

As I sat down and started to talk business with my new

client, I was amazed to see the dog calmly cock its leg against the superb seventeeth century Queen Anne table which stood near the window. Mrs Franklin's face reddened as she saw the wet table leg and the unsightly stain on her luxurious Axminster carpet, but she made no comment. I was feeling puzzled and slightly uneasy, as I just could not reconcile the refined hostess with her immaculate bungalow on the one hand, with the rather dirty and distinctly badly-behaved dog on the other. However, dog owners are a diverse lot in my experience, so I thought no more of it and proceeded with our discussion.

A few minutes later, after I had finished giving her my legal advice, I got up from my chair to go to the door, but before I had reached it I was appalled to notice the dog making a rather more serious call of nature, this time right in the middle of the Persian hearth rug. Mrs Franklin's face was a mixture of anger, disbelief and embarrassment.

As I shook hands with her at the door, she had one final question to ask me.

'Aren't you taking your dog with you, Mr Francis?'

'It's not mine, Mrs Franklin', I replied and then added without thinking: 'I assumed it was yours.'

I immediately realised my mistake.

'Mr Francis, you surely didn't believe that dirty, smelly dog was mine, did you? What sort of a person do you think I am?'

She then burst into floods of tears and slammed the front door shut.

I never did discover the owner of that badly-behaved sheepdog, but I should like to meet that person to exchange a few choice words, because he or she lost me a very good client that day.

When I was a boy, this was the month I always looked out for the change in the type of moths, clouds of which used to flutter into the car headlights on any evening journey. I watched them carefully as the winter varieties vanished, to be replaced by what have always been called the 'early moths', which were followed in turn by the frail and fragile little March moths. It is sad to reflect that it is not only our native butterflies which are becoming scarcer these days but also our moths, for the clouds of them which used to appear in car headlights are now but a distant memory.

I have never been quite so interested in moths as in butterflies, but there are still certain species which, whenever I come across them, bring back memories and associations with my boyhood. The magpie moth which I used to disturb among raspberries and gooseberry bushes, the yellow underwing which would fly up as I crawled among the straw of the strawberry bed, the handsome emperor moth which I used to breed up from caterpillars found on the drab moor opposite Dick Hudsons, the garden tiger moth which I used to breed in the bathroom cupboard (much to my mother's consternation) from caterpillars which we children used to call 'woolly bears', and most memorable and evocative of all the five spot burnet moth, black, dotted in red and day-flying, which I shall always associate with holidays at Filey.

Here there was – and as far as I know still is – a large dark type of the species quite different to its smaller, paler inland relative. The revered fathers of British entomology have now decided in their wisdom that they are one and the same species, but to me the Filey form will always be special and separate, and will forever be associated in my mind with all the other happy memories of that delightful Yorkshire resort: donkey rides, seabathing, buckets and spades and digging sandcastles, inspecting the ruts on the beach to see whether the proposed 'Test Match' cricket pitch would take spin, being cross with my sister when she dropped a sitter at backward short leg off my bowling, watching my mother and my friends' mothers running endless rounders, hearing the sound of the breakers and of children laughing and crying, slithering and slipping among the rock pools on Filey Brigg, trying to dress and undress with some degree of modesty in the old-fashioned beach huts, eating ice cream and picnicking on the beach and trying to persuade the wasps to go somewhere else, going back to our boarding house where there was in those days the rather peculiar arrangement whereby the landlady cooked the food which was chosen and bought by her guests, and all of these things going on underneath the wild and unspoilt cliffs, home of the Filey burnet moth.

Whilst I was looking out for the change of moths outside the office, inside I was hoping to chance upon a case which would provide some light relief amid the dreary days.

I guessed I had found such a case when George and Elinor Dixon called in to see me one day. Now they were two people I was always pleased to see, because although they never had much money they were both so cheerful – George in particular always had a twinkle in his eye and a rare sense of humour.

They were both in their sixties now, and had barely enough money to live on ever since the day some years ago when George was disabled as a result of falling off a tractor on the Dales farm where he had worked since leaving school. His disability pension was topped up by his wife doing a little cleaning work, but all in all they were poor, very poor.

However, George and Elinor had hopes that one day they would be rich, because they were beneficiaries of a trust fund which would be theirs absolutely upon the death of their distant cousin Joseph. Now Joseph, who was entitled to the income from the trust fund for his lifetime, was about the same age as George and Elinor, but what gave them both some hope was the fact that he was a chronic alcoholic.

When I had advised them on the small matter of business they had wanted to discuss, George said rather apologetically to me:

'Ah knows we're not reet good clients for thee, Mr Francis, but 'appen one day we'll be rich an' then tha'll be pleased to work for us.'

I realised from George's grin that he was referring to the possible demise of his cousin Joseph.

'Have you heard anything of Joseph of late?', I enquired.

'Aye, well 'e allus sends us a Christmas card dus cousin Joseph, but Ah reckon t' writin' on it were a bit more shaky, like, this year.'

'Do you send him anything for Christmas?', I asked.

There was a pause as George looked at Elinor, winked at her and then tried to keep a straight face as he replied.

'Well, t' missus an' me reckoned t' job up, an' bethought us that t' best present we could give cousin Joseph would be a large crate o' whisky – to 'elp t' job along, like. What dus tha reckon to t' notion?'

'You didn't really...', I began.

'Nay, Mr Francis, Ah'm only pullin' yer leg. But tha's got to admit that it'd be a reet grand way for 'im to go, like, an' it'd be jus' t' job for t' missus an' me, an' all.'

I am constantly surprised by the youthfulness, energy and enthusiasm of some of my friends and business acquaintances who are old in years, but young in spirit. They put to shame many of their contemporaries, whose attitudes and physical appearance make them prematurely old.

I have told before of my tennis friend Wilf, who at the age of seventy-four still plays the game, winter and summer alike, with tremendous skill and enthusiasm; there is my business executive friend Peter, who at the age of fifty-three still turns out regularly for the fourth team at Denley Rugby Club; and there are many sprightly ladies in the dale in their seventies and eighties who attend keep-fit classes, go dancing and embark on trips all over the world. But one perishing cold day this month I met a chap called Reg Farnhill during a day's beagling up on the moors, and to my mind he capped the lot of them.

Whilst I struggled to keep pace with this octogenarian as he made light of following the hounds, climbing over walls, gates and styles, and tramped easily over miles of heather-clad moorland and russet-coloured bracken, he casually mentioned, in between pointing out lapwings, golden plovers, curlews and grouse which his still sharp eyes had spotted, that this ten mile run was a bit of light training to help keep him fit for the two games of squash he still played against a fellow octogenarian every week.

Age is, I think, very much a matter of mind and attitude. You are as young as you feel. The trick is to keep your interests and enthusiasms wherever they lie. 'Never give up', as Churchill said, or as my octogenarian, beagling, squash-playing friend Reg put it rather more expressively:

'Tha's got to keep buggerin' on, lad.'

It is usually towards the end of February each year when I resolve to put my books into some kind of order and to catalogue them properly, but somehow my best intentions always seem to go astray.

The bookshelves which house my collection of country and Yorkshire books are generally in reasonable order, for they are the ones I read most often: Jefferies and Hudson, White and Cobbett; John Moore, prophet and conservationist ahead of his time, whose last book *The Waters under the Earth* is in my opinion one of the greatest country novels of all time; Adrian Bell, father of TV reporter Martin Bell, whose trilogy *Corduroy*, *Silver Ley* and *The Cherry Tree* contains prose of the most exquisite delicacy; Henry Williamson, reviled for his fascist views but author of the best amimal stories I have ever read; Hugh Massingham, Ian Niall, B B, and A G Street. They are all fine country writers to whom I return again and again.

There are so many good books about Yorkshire and Yorkshire people, but if I had to make a choice then I think the favourite authors on my shelves would have to be J S Fletcher, J B Priestley, Bogg, Speight, Willie Riley, and perhaps most evocative of all in terms of character and place, the Dales books written by Marie Hartley with her co-authors, first Ella Pontefract until her untimely death and since then with Joan Ingilby.

The country books and Yorkshire books can stay where they are. It is the other miscellaneous books which I never seem to sort out, but I am not sure whether it is wholly desirable anyway, for there is something rather comforting if bizarre in finding my old *Boys Book of Soccer* for 1949 next to Mrs Beeton's book on jam-making, my complete works of Shakespeare being kept immediate company by my Biggles books, and a treasured volume on the history of the fly rod being propped up by an unread book about travel in ancient Palestine!

Perhaps next year I will really put my books in order...but somehow I doubt it.

Farmers and farming ways change like the rest of us, but they perhaps change more slowly and, particularly among the older generation, old-fashioned attitudes die hard.

Fred Hellifield is a good example of the type, and has been for as many years as I can remember. I was glad to get in from the cold one day towards the back end of the month, as Fred opened the door and ushered me into the kitchen of his farmhouse, cosily situated in a dip in the moors above Denley. Fred went straight back to his favourite armchair by the fire, sat back and stretched out his feet.

'Na then, missus', he shouted out to his long-suffering wife Mary who was not in the room. 'There's Mr Francis t' solicitor 'ere, jus' fetch 'im a chair through will yer.'

I immediately offered to bring it myself, but Fred would have none of it. I stood rather embarrassed as Mary staggered into the kitchen with a large armchair which she placed at the other side of the fire. Fred made absolutely no acknowledgement of his wife's efforts, but carried on talking to me as Mary sat down on an old wooden chair at the kitchen table. There was a minute's silence and Fred turned to his 'missus' again.

'It's a dry ship is this, luv.'

Up jumped Mary without a word. The next thing I heard was the unmistakable sound of tea being made in the small room next door. Mary had hardly put the tea tray down before us when Fred turned to me and said:

'Na then Mr Francis, tha reckoned to want to look at t' deeds.'

I nodded. Mary was already halfway to the large bureau-cum-kitchen-cupboard as her husband said:

'Reet missus, jus' fetch us t' deeds from t' cupboard will yer.'

Fred was still sitting comfortably and drinking his tea as I examined the deeds which Mary had handed to me. I gave Fred my opinion

31

concerning a right of way which was referred to somewhat ambiguously in an old handwritten conveyance of 1863, and then I gently reminded him of a bill of mine which had been outstanding for over eighteen months and which he had promised to pay when I visited him. He didn't say a word to me, but grunted as he turned once again to his wife .

'Fetch us t' cheque book, lass, for Mr Francis.'

Mary once again scurried away to do her husband's bidding, and as she handed the cheque book to him, he frowned at her and said:

'Nay, woman, gie it tae Mr Francis, 'e can write t' cheque out for us an' Ah'll sign it, like.'

Mary let out a resigned sort of sigh, gave me the cheque book and left the room.

I left the farm shortly afterwards with Fred's cheque lodged safely in my back pocket. As I did so I reflected on the scene I had just witnessed, a scene which was comical in a way and yet one which would appall any modern-day feminist, that of the dominant husband and the obedient, unquestioning wife; embarrassing in a way, yet I knew that Fred and Mary were devoted to each other and that divorce in the farming community is still unusual. As Fred once put it to me:

'Round 'ere, Mr Francis, Ah reckons that men are still men an' t' women are glad of 'em.'

On the last day of the month I drove home from the office in daylight, and I stood for a few minutes in the garden contemplating the view of the dale, the fields silent apart from the bleating of a few early lambs, the river still in spate from the melting snow and the church clock striking the hour in the distance.

'God's own country', I reflected, as my eyes followed the landscape from the horizon of the heather moors above me down the dale from my own home – a Victorian farmhouse set in the middle of the small village of Wathvale – to the market town of Denley, with its surrounding farms and smallholdings, its churches and chapels, its fine cricket ground, its pubs, its small shops and its warm-hearted people.

There would be rough days in March no doubt, but as I closed the garden gate and went into the house for a pot of tea – so refreshing after a day's work – I reckoned that the worst of the winter was over, that snow if it came would not stay long, and that the coming of spring was at hand.

Chapter Three

> ' . . . daffodils
> That come before the swallow dares and take
> The winds of March with beauty . . . '
> William Shakespeare

March, it has always been said, roars in like a lion and goes out like a lamb, the violent winds at the beginning of the month giving way to deceptively balmy days later on, when you are liable to catch cold if you don't wrap up properly.

There are some splendid walks only a stone's throw from my home. On the first fine Saturday of the month I make for one of my favourites, which starts just above Wathvale village.

It is good to feel the wind on my face as I walk up Silver Hill, and contemplate the view of Cuckoo Wood above and the river still running in spate through the dale below. It is a wind which cleanses the mind, blowing away the cobwebs of the long dreary days and the depression of winter. My spirit starts to lift as I anticipate flowers and fishing, butterflies and birdsong. Close by the top of the hill is a field where already there are a few peewits flying, and in a few weeks' time when they are nesting and guarding their young I can expect to

33

be dive-bombed, particularly if I am accompanied by my dog. As I listen to the call of the peewit, I realise that it is one of those birds which names itself.

They are not the only birds to see on this wild day. On the moor above Silver Hill, there are lapwings, golden plovers and grouse, whilst on the way down I hear the distinctive call of the curlew, before my attention is caught by a sparrowhawk soaring above a field near to the river where there are always rabbits in plenty.

I like to make a start in the garden this month. I had already pruned and forked, cleared away the dead growth and had a bonfire. In fact I thought I was doing very well until I decided to buy some fish meal as an activator for the compost heap. As my own car was being repaired at the garage, I used Rosemary's car. Unfortunately the bag of fish meal broke just as I was getting out, spilling the contents all over the inside of the car.

'Whatever is that awful smell in my car?', asked Rosemary the next day, after she had been out shopping.

'I'm afraid I have a confession to make', I replied.

I had done my best to clean up the car, but to my knowledge there is no smell which is more persistent and lingering than that of fish meal. I fear Rosemary will have to endure it for some months to come.

I was trying very hard not to smile about this prospect as I forked the herbaceous border, accompanied by one of our semi-tame robins which stood, head cocked on one side, waiting for juicy worms to appear. As I moved on from the herbaceous border to do all the other jobs which a gardener must do at this time of year, and as muscles, atrophied by winter inactivity, started to function again, so, as I looked around the garden and the dale below, did the natural world seem to awaken after its winter hibernation.

'It's the end of an era', said local accountant Leslie Storey, as we walked away together from Denley Church after the funeral service of our good friend Charles Vernon, family doctor in Denley and its surrounding villages for over forty years.

Family doctors, like family solicitors, are a fast vanishing species. Certainly we shall not see the likes of Dr Vernon again, friend, physician and father confessor to generations of Denley folk.

'I will not talk about cases', he once said to me, 'a case is a container. I look after people.'

Possessed of a great sense of humour, Charles had cheerfully practised medicine in a manner characterised by conscientiousness and Yorkshire common sense. Although a man of great compassion, he was not inclined to waste much sympathy upon malingerers. In this respect he reminded me very much of my old school doctor, a Scotsman called Bill Aird whose standard prescription for boys hoping to stay off school for a while was 'up today and out tomorrow, that's the very thing'. There's another response which many modern-day doctors favour whatever the nature of the patient's complaint – 'It's a virus'. I often wish there was a similar statement which solicitors could make to cover all their clients' ills!

I've noticed, too, that doctors have another trick from which solicitors could arguably learn, that of transferring concern for their patients' condition to their own medical problems and history.

There was a certain Dales doctor, now long dead, who perfected this particular technique. It was said of him, perhaps rather unkindly, that he was only capable of accurately diagnosing two human conditions – namely birth and death. Whatever his patients complained about, he had always suffered from the disease himself. He would regale his patients at length with an account of the time he was laid up for six months with backache, or of when he collapsed with a duodenal ulcer, or of the agonising period when he suffered from shingles, whilst his patient waited in vain for some sympathy, concern or prognosis for his own condition. Whatever his patient's complaint, the good doctor had suffered from it himself – and much more severely.

Talking about him one day Alf Raygill, one of the more colourful Dales characters, made a remark which my old friend Dr Charles Vernon would surely have appreciated:

'Yon bugger 'ud be fair capped if Ah went in theer and tell'd 'im Ah were pregnant'!

It is the first warm sunny day of the month, and I have been looking for those landmarks of spring which somehow become more important and precious as the years go by. At any rate, I have seen my first small tortoiseshell butterfly, a female, looking surprisingly fresh after her long winter hibernation. I have also seen the first pied wagtail in the garden, the first bees foraging for pollen and the first celandines in flower.

Apart from celandines, there are two flowers which I particularly associate with March, namely the marsh marigold and the butterbur.

There was a meadow near my boyhood home through which there ran a small stream, and my sister and I used to walk there just to see the marsh marigolds which grew there in profusion. We always went in our wellies for the land was what 'Owd Jacob' always described as 'groshy', a lovely onomatopoeic dialect word from up Wharfedale meaning boggy or marshy. When I recall that 'groshy' piece of land, with its deceptive carpet of bright golden yellow, I smile to myself as I remember from my student days a certain case involving an estate agent who was sued by an irate purchaser who discovered that some land which he had just bought, and which had been described by that same estate agent as 'an uncommon fine water meadow', turned out to be a swamp!

The butterburs I used to find in plenty near the riverbank on Castley Lane. Near to these rather squat, purpled and hyacinth-like flowers, and the small tortoiseshell butterflies which flew around them, was a dipper and sand martin-haunted beck which ran under a little bridge before joining the river. There were minnows in that beck, which we boys used to catch in jam jars with bread at the bottom and a small hole at the top, and also sticklebacks which were universally known as 'tiddlers'.

Whenever I see March sunshine, in my mind I am a boy again cycling along Castley Lane with a carefree spirit and anticipating seeing the first small tortoiseshell of the year, the butterburs and the small fishes and being filled with a sense of wonder, adventure and the magic of things.

I am still thinking of marsh marigolds and butterburs and Castley Lane as I contemplate my garden and the countryside beyond, brightened as it is by the sunshine of early spring. As I 'car quiet', as 'Owd Jacob' would have said, I hear all the familiar and well-loved sounds of the dale – a tractor making its way down the lane, a distant shepherd's whistle, the river still running in spate, the bleating of early lambs and a skylark singing.

Clients come and go, but some keep turning up like the proverbial bad penny. There is old Ernest, who has already changed his will four times, even though the year is not three months old; there is Sharon, whose husband Wayne keeps assaulting her on a Saturday night after drinking too much ale, who regularly instructs me to file for divorce but always becomes reconciled to her husband before the papers are served; and there is Richard, known to his friends as 'Tricky Dicky', who specialises in claiming against insurance companies for various 'accidents' to his person and property. 'Must get my premiums back, you know', he was once heard to say to a friend.

But the client of the year was obviously destined to be 'Lucky Jim' Bottomley. He had no success when he came to see me with his story of the ill-starred ride in the sports car, and I wondered what it was that had brought him back to my office so soon. I didn't have to wait long to find out. I already knew what his first word was likely to be, and I was not disappointed.

'*Un*fortunately, Ah've lost some brass, Mr Francis, an' Ah'm lookin' to thee to git it back for us.'

I knew I was in for another tale of woe, to be told at length and in excruciating detail. I tried to bring him to the point but without success, so I just leaned back in my chair and listened as his tale unfolded.

'Nay, Mr Francis, tha wants to know t' job frae t' start, Ah reckons. It were like this yer see. Ah were tellin' t' missus that it were aboot time she gave me t' job of lookin' after t' brass she'd cum into after 'er Uncle George died, but – an' this tha'll surely find 'ard to reckon up, Mr Francis – t' lass didn't seem reet keen on t' idea. Anyroad, she came round to my way o' thinkin' in t' finish, an' theer Ah were wi' ten thousand pund to invest. T' missus jus' said to me, "I'm sick to death of you goin' on about it, here it is and just you make sure that you look after it for us". Well, Mr Francis, Ah took me time an' were reet careful to find t' best spot to put t' brass. After a bit Ah saw this advertisement, like, frae a company in t' paper which were offerin' near double what t' missus could've gitten in t' buildin' society. So Ah puts t' lot in wi' 'em an' waits for t' fust dividend. "Ah reckon tha'll be reet suited wi' this investment Ah've med for thee", Ah said to t' missus. Anyroad, Mr Francis, an' Ah'd best tell thee straight, *un*fortunately Ah nivver 'ad no dividend, and na there's a letter landed this mornin', like, frae a feller callin' himself a liquidator or summat o' t' soart – is 'e lookin' after t' job for us now?'

'I've got some bad news for you, Mr Bottomley. The liquidator has been called in because the company you've invested in is insolvent. You'll be lucky to get tuppence in the pound.'

A quick telephone call from me confirmed this, and that the directors were in police custody on suspicion of fraud.

'Nothing I can do for you, Mr Bottomley. You've lost the money and I don't envy you having to tell your wife.'

'Nay, Mr Francis, that's t' least part o' t' job. T' lass 'll weigh t' job up an' own that t' idea were reet. Ah were jus' *un*fortunate, like, in t' company Ah chose.'

There are some matters upon which solicitors are consulted which are of very great importance, involving for instance a possible loss of liberty, a driving disqualification, a crucial business transaction or where a large sum of money is at stake. There are, by contrast, other cases which lie at the opposite end of the spectrum.

I was presented with such a case this month when a widow called Norma Jones came in to see me. She waved in my face a letter she had just received from the council threatening to take legal proceedings against her – for the princely sum of fifty pence.

Now Norma, who lives by herself in a flat, one of a number which form a block of sheltered accommodation provided by the council for the elderly, had attempted to make a call from the telephone which the council had provided for the residents' communal use. For some reason she could not get through, and when she tried to retrieve her fifty pence piece she was unable to do so. After her initial fury had subsided, she thought she had hit upon the perfect solution. She simply deducted fifty pence from her rates. The council had failed to accept her 'solution', and had now threatened to put her in court as a rates defaulter.

'I must admit that it seems a neat way of resolving the matter, but it won't work in law', I advised her.

I thought you'd say that', she replied, 'it's a bugger i'n't it?'

As I showed Norma out of the office and reflected on her parting shot, I was reminded of 'old Wilkie', a former client of mine who died many years ago. A local character, Wilkie – John Septimus Wilkinson Brown to give him his proper name – always dressed in the same old suit, wore a battered old trilby hat and carried a tatty umbrella. He was well-known for his careful attitude to money, and his favourite expression, amongst other rather riper ones, was 'it's a bugger'.

Stories about Wilkie are still legion, and are told and retold by Dales folk. There was the time he stood watching out of his window as the local woodyard delivered five bags of kindling. Wilkie insisted that he had only received four, and the unfortunate driver had to gather up the wood and re-bag it to prove to him that he had received his full quota and must pay for it accordingly.

There were times without number when worshippers sharing the same pew as him in church had seen him pretend to put money in the collection plate. And there were stories from all the local dealers in town that he was prone to haunt charity shops, church bazaars and charity stalls, with a view to picking up books and bric-a-brac cheaply and then selling them on for an immediate profit.

The last time I had seen Wilkie alive was when I was in the local supermarket. I was suddenly aware of a sharp stabbing pain in my back. I turned round and there was old Wilkie, wielding his tatty but lethal black umbrella which he had so painfully prodded into the small of my back.

'Hello, Wilkie', I said with as much cheerfulness as I could muster in the circumstances.

'It's a bugger when you can't reach t' shelves', he said.

Those were his last words to me before he died, and I suppose that is why it is an expression which has stayed in my mind.

Wilkie's favourite expression came to mind again as I surveyed my garden one day late in the month after a particularly windy night. The daffodils bought in a job lot from Woolworths fifteen years ago – and amazingly good value ever since – were bent almost to the ground, some of my hybrid tea roses were victims of wind rock, and the drain in the wind tunnel which is our drive was full of leaves and needed unblocking.

I came to terms with playing tennis in the wind long ago when I was at school, for there were always stiff sea breezes at Rossall. I think I have now just about accepted working in an exposed and windy garden, slogging up and down the steep slope to cultivate borders and rockeries, striving to establish plants in the most favourable position (surely the key to successful gardening), constantly retying plants which have come adrift from their supports, and generally trying to keep flowers which do not like wind as happy as possible. Difficulties generally bring compensations, and this gardener will cheerfully accept the problems of gardening in a windy and exposed climate when he is blessed daily with a grand view over the dale.

As I contemplated the damage caused in the garden by the wind, I started to reckon up all the jobs which needed doing. It is as well that gardeners are philosophers, for otherwise they would be constantly outfaced. There were the lawns to cut, roses and shrubs to prune, borders and rockeries to be weeded and tidied, raspberries – which

I should have tipped in February – to be retied and mucked, the vegetable plot to be prepared and the annual ritual of the fruit trees to be completed.

At this time of year there is one job in the garden which I have always done if I have done nothing else, and that is to weed and clean around the apple, pear and plum trees. It is a practice which many would not think necessary or important, but it is an ancient one, having been recommended by Virgil in *The Georgics* if I remember rightly from reading Latin at school.

As I stood contemplating the tasks which lay before me, I was aware that the warm sunshine of earlier days in the month had brought about some precocious flowering, and after the reckoning by the wind there was a danger of further damage by late frosts. A gardener has to start somewhere, and I decided quite irrationally that my first job would be to sort out a very untidy Dorothy Perkins rambler rose at the top of my drive. This lovely, old-fashioned, pink-clustered rambling rose had been neglected, and was in need of radical surgery as well as a good load of muck spreading around it.

As I wheeled my barrow of muck up to the top of the drive, I spotted a man just passing my garden gate whom I recognised as Jason Edwards, a businessman in Denley. He looked at me for a second, turned away and then looked at me again, but this time with a double take which would have graced the stage of our local dramatic society. He had, I suppose, seen me previously when I was at the office or in court, dressed in a smart business suit. I could see him trying to weigh up in his mind whether the man standing before him in an old donkey jacket, corduroys, boots, and with a muck-splattered face really could be his solicitor.

'Mr Francis, is it?', he asked somewhat hesitantly.

Out of context, a solicitor can be almost incognito, I later thought to myself. There's a lesson in that somewhere.

Quite a large amount of a solicitor's time is spent searching for, looking out and examining title deeds and documents. Looking at an old handwritten conveyance which lay right at the bottom of a packet of deeds one day this month, it reminded me how much conveyancing practice in a lawyer's office has changed over the years. The days when a managing clerk laboriously and beautifully wrote out deeds by hand, and when his principal spent perhaps a whole day attending to just one completion, which was sealed with the client over a glass of sherry, have gone forever. It has just been decreed that seals themselves are no longer necessary. In the old days, a party to a deed would place his thumb over the seal and say out loud in the presence of a witness: 'I deliver this as my act and deed'.

One of the managing clerk's principal duties was to prepare what was called 'an abstract of title', a précis or summary of the various documents which linked together to form a chain of ownership or legal title. Abstracting a title is a lost and forgotten art. I doubt whether any young solicitor or legal executive nowadays would know how to attempt it. They simply photocopy the relevant documents instead.

Without doubt, the advent of the photocopier has been the biggest single change in solicitors' offices during my time in the law. It abolished the need for copy typists at a stroke, but like all the other modern inventions in the office it suffers the disadvantage of being seriously abused. Prior to its coming, solicitors had to give very careful thought as to which documents would actually be needed for a case; the tendency now is for solicitors to take the easy option of photocopying everything in sight, whether relevant or not.

Not only is this widespread practice very wasteful of paper, but it also to explains why trials are often so lengthy and expensive. Barristers are often long-winded by nature, but when their cases are document-cluttered they have a ready excuse for their verbal diarrhoea!

Even the telephone, which has been with us for many years, is badly abused – a high proportion of calls, I am sure, would on analysis be found unnecessary; the computer is used as a universal excuse for anything which ever goes wrong in an office; and the word processor provides endless opportunities for lawyers to churn out lengthy documents unaccompanied by any thought or application to the matter in hand.

But of all the modern technology and gadgetry with which we now have to work, my particular *bête noire* is the fax machine, a useful facility in itself but one which is heaven-sent for the inefficient, disorganised solicitor who always leaves everything until the last moment. There is nothing in the office which irritates me more than receiving a fax from another solicitor, asking a question which he should have raised a month earlier, and demanding an instant reply by fax.

It is no wonder that the pace and pressure of office life have dramatically increased, particularly when you ally the effect of office technology to the ever-present demands these days for jobs to be all done and dusted the day before yesterday!

Solicitors, I reflect more and more frequently, are in danger of becoming just like the dealers and market makers in the city, spending their working lives sitting in front of computer screens, slaves to technology and gadgetry, subject to continued pressure anxiety and stress, and completely burnt out by the age of thirty!

Bertie Smith is a farming client of mine, and one I have always learnt to treat with the greatest possible respect. As a bachelor he has always had plenty of time to study different aspects of matters which concern him on his farm, and consequently he always has an answer for everyone. He had little formal education and is completely self-taught, but I learnt long ago to underestimate his knowledge of the law at my peril. For Bertie knows all about the Agricultural Holdings Act, the difference between tenancies and grazing agreements, the laws governing notices to quit and the rules of good husbandry, about subsidies and quotas, and about the effect of the latest Common Market regulations.

I went to see Bertie one day late in the month to discuss a proposed new will and a tax-saving scheme. After I had explained rather laboriously one or two matters relating to inheritance tax, he interrupted me and said impatiently:

'Nay, Mr Francis, Ah knows all about that.'

It became clear during the discussion which followed that he was indeed fully conversant with inheritance tax, agricultural and retirement relief, and holdover concessions – as well as with the different tax bands, potentially exempt transfers, annual exemptions and marriage gifts.

To cap it all, he had produced his own tax-saving scheme, taking all the factors into account which I had so carefully explained.

'Na don't jus' stand theer lookin' capped, Mr Francis, will it do, d'yer reckon?'

I felt humble, but I knew I was in good company.

It was not just lawyers he kept up to the mark. For many years Bertie had been the terror of council representatives, agricultural

42

advisers and planning officials, who had found to their cost that if they had not been up very early in the day to do their homework properly, Bertie would run rings round them.

The tales about Bertie are legion. To his doctor who said to him after prescribing a course of tablets, 'I hope you feel better after a few days, Mr Smith', he replied 'Ah bloody 'ope so an all'.

When the doctor visited him a week later and enquired whether the tablets had done the trick, Bertie replied:

'Nay, doctor, t' best spot for them tablets were straight down t' drain, but don't fret thisen, Ah've fettled mysen wi' t' medicine me gran'father allus used.'

To a financial salesman, who spent half an hour trying to sell him some unit trusts and extolling their likely profitability, he listened patiently before shaking his head, putting his hand on the young man's shoulder and saying:

'Nay lad, if t' job's gitten that much brass in it, tha'd 've med tha fortune an' as sure as 'ell tha'd be livin' t' life o' Reilly – an' not be forced to do what tha's reckonin' to do now.'

To a vet who had been unable to cure some sheep which appeared listless and unfit, he said after the vet had finally admitted failure:

'Reight, vitnary, theer's one way o' fettlin' yon sick yows that's nivver failed us yet. Cum back in a fortneet an' tek a look at 'em.'

The vet came back two weeks later, and was amazed to see the same sheep grazing contentedly, apparently cured. Bertie turned to him and said:

'Ah tell thee, vitnary, all them yows were short of were a week or two on sum fresh 'erby grass in yon medder.'

The vet shook his head and looked nonplussed.

'It's just experience, yer see, vitnary.'

But of all the stories about Bertie, my favourite is about the time he was visited on his farm by an evangelist who was endeavouring to spread the word to the remotest corners of the countryside.

After a long journey up the dale, he made his way along the bumpy track which led to Bertie's farm. He had to stop seven times to open and close gates, but eventually parked in the farmyard next to some junky old tractors and piles of scrap metal lying among clumps of nettles.

As the grizzled old farmer came to the door to greet him, the evangelist said:

'Have you ever read the Bible?'

Bertie thought carefully:

'Aye lad, Ah've read t' Bible.'

'Well', said the evangelist, thinking it would be a good moment to introduce the subject of animals as it was a farmer he was trying to convert, 'have you read the story about Noah and his ark?'

Bertie thought again for a moment, looked solemnly at the preacher and then replied:

'Aye, Ah've read all about Noah an' t' ark an' t'beasts goin' in two by two. But', he said as he continued to look the evangelist straight in the face with a deadly serious expression, 'what Ah wants to know is – an' 'appen thee can tell us – who were t' poor divil who 'ad to muck 'em all out?'

Chapter Four

'Whan that Aprille with his shoures sote
The droughte of March hath perced to the rote.'
Geoffrey Chaucer

April is traditionally the month for romance, being named after Aphro, a short form of Aphrodite, the Goddess of Love. But wherever the thoughts of young men may turn to at this time of year, when the first April shower comes along I always think of Chaucer. I had to learn his *Prologue to the Canterbury Tales* for my GCE English examination, and my English master, a great Chaucer enthusiast, insisted that we all had to recite his work in fourteenth century English. To this end he acquired a tape recording of *The Prologue* spoken by a famous professional actor, whom we were all expected to copy.

So when the sweet winds and soft showers which characterise the lovely month of April sweep across the dale, and I listen to the birds singing in the garden, I reflect that the pilgrims on their way to Canterbury six centuries ago felt exactly the same pleasure and joy in the coming of spring – the time of year when 'smale fowles maken melodye'.

As I stand by the garden gate in the still of the evening and look up the dale, there seems scarcely a field without sheep, and as I listen to the bleating of their lambs I think of the beautiful recording of *All in an April evening* by the Glasgow Orpheus choir. As my mind turns to poetry and music I remember Shakespeare's description of the month, 'well-apparelled and proud-pied', but best of all for me are the words from *I sing of a maiden*:

> 'He came all so stille
> Where his mother was
> As dew in Aprille
> That falleth on the grass.'

45

Can it really be two years ago since I listened with increasing emotion to my youngest son singing these lovely lines in a clear treble voice in his school chapel? School plays and concerts can be very emotional experiences for parents, and in this context I think nativity plays take a lot of beating. Rosemary and I watched our three children for what seemed countless years as they all graduated from being stars to angels to shepherds, and finally to being Joseph or Mary. We were by no means the only parents with hankies close to hand, but there were lighter moments in these productions, as for instance on the occasion when 'Mary' made her entrance, came full centre stage, burst into tears and sobbed:

'I want my Mummy.'

Next to the garden gate where I am standing and contemplating the view up the dale, is a clump of that delightful old-fashioned plant honesty in full flower; on the other side is an old damson tree in blossom, from which earlier in the day had risen the steady hum of bees; whilst among the fruit trees beyond, a single chaffinch is singing.

April is a lovely name for a lovely month, and as I reluctantly leave the garden at twilight to come indoors I find myself instinctively reciting Robert Browing's delightful sonnet *Home Thoughts from Abroad* with its immortal first lines:

'Oh to be in England,
Now that April's there'

It is generally about this time of year when our probate practice starts to pick up, as people who have struggled and just held on through the winter succumb to the effects of their efforts.

Indeed the month had hardly begun, when I found myself attending the funeral service of Archie Scriven, friend, local character and long-standing client of mine. The service was to be followed by a private burial for the family only in the village churchyard. I came out of church and called in to see William the gravedigger, whom I have known since childhood and whose cottage was only a hundred yards from the churchyard.

William had just handed me a mug of tea and we had started chatting about the state of the world in general and about his village in particular, when our conversation was interrupted in the most dramatic way. There was a loud and frenzied hammering on

46

the door and, before William could open it, Fred Dalton, the local joiner and undertaker burst in, his face red and sweaty, his black funeral garb dishevelled and his expression one of acute anxiety and distress. Before William could say 'What's up?', Fred exclaimed in a voice which combined panic, embarrassment and despair:

'Nay, William, t' coffin won't drop.'

William reacted to this startling statement with a calm and measured disbelief.

'Well, Ah measured t' job reet enuff – is tha sure, Mr Dalton?'

'Ah wouldn't be standin' 'ere now if Ah wasn't sure, William. T' relations are all round t' grave now, waitin' for t'coffin to drop. Tha'd best cum up now.'

The two men left quickly.

Despite the solemnity of the occasion, and the distress which must have been caused to Archie's family standing round the grave as their beloved one failed to 'lie down', I couldn't help but smile to myself at Fred's predicament. Not wanting to appear morbidly curious, I decided not to follow the two men but to await William's return. It was only a few minutes before he was back.

'Well?', I said, eager to know what had transpired.

'Nay, Mr Francis, Ah'd measured t' job reet enuff. It were just a small pebble that 'ud dropped down t' side and were holdin' t' coffin fast wheer it were.'

The irony in this little happening lay in the fact that Archie, who had so dramatically refused to 'lie down', had been during his lifetime a great character who loved telling tales at his local pub, particularly about undertakers. He would, I am sure, have appreciated as a last joke being told the story of 't' coffin that wouldn't drop'.

I was telling a solicitor friend of mine in Lancashire about this event shortly afterwards, and he in turn related an experience of his at a funeral which had caused his firm great embarrassment.

A client of his, known to all as Uncle Joe, had died. As sole executor and there being no close relatives, he had been asked to arrange the funeral. Due to some misunderstanding, my friend had gained the impression from the family that there was very little money in the estate, and he took it into his head that the funeral should be the cheapest and most basic available. He therefore instructed the local undertaker accordingly.

On the day of the funeral, the deceased's relatives and friends waiting at the church were aghast to see a little green joiner's van

arrive, with Uncle Joe's coffin lying in a distinctly undignified position in the back, scarcely visible among the joiner's tools and bits of wood.

It turned out that there was over £50,000 in Uncle Joe's estate, and the family had certainly not expected or wanted such a parsimonious approach to his funeral. I would imagine that my solicitor friend had an awful lot of letters of apology to write.

In favoured villages like Linton near Wetherby, garden rockeries are generally in flower as early as March, but here in the Dales it is April or sometimes even May before they are at their best. There is so much to do in the garden at this time of year that I rarely have time to appreciate mine. This, I always think, is a pity, for the spectacle of a garden rockery in full bloom is one over which a gardener should linger.

At any rate, one Saturday morning I find a few minutes to pause and enjoy the sight of my own rockery just approaching its best: the flowers, lit by the spring sunshine, are a glorious combination of colours – purple and pink aubretia, yellow alyssum, white candytuft, red and white clumps of saxifrage, many-coloured lungwort, london pride and primulas – and, wafting towards me in the breeze, is the heady scent of wallflowers.

As I look around the garden, in odd gaps and forgotten nooks, crannies and neglected corners, the forget-me-not has seeded itself. This pretty blue flower, along with other corner fillers like the welsh poppy, and heartsease – the tiny wild pansy – paint a picture which in its own way is as pretty as any cultivated rockery.

Looking at my watch, I see that I have just enough time to walk down to the river before lunch. The fields through which I walk are full of the yellow flowers I always associate with spring – coltsfoot, celandines, and dandelions – and in a matter of weeks the dale will be golden with buttercups, 'the little children's flower'.

I do not know of a bank locally 'whereon the wild thyme blows', as Shakespeare did, but between the river and small wood below our house there is a grassy and partly-wooded slope, where at this time of year two of my favourite spring flowers, violets and primroses, are in full flower. The sweet-scented violets with their heart-shaped leaves, surely emblems of love, are perfectly complemented by the delicate yellow primroses with their scent of earth and of woodland. I shall always associate these two flowers, for they surely go together just like buttercups and daisies, or poppies and peonies.

At the far side of the bank is an area of marshy ground, a good spot for the green-veined white, a butterfly which should soon be on the wing, and beyond that is a small pond where now there is a frothy mass of frogspawn, and where later in the year there will be dragonflies.

Looking at frogspawn always brings back memories, for it was an annual ritual when I was a boy to collect and take home a bucketful of this fascinating substance, and then watch the development of the tadpoles from the tiny specks inside the eggs; first the tail, then the back legs, then the front pair and later on, as the legs grew, watching the tail shrink, disappear and finally turn into a baby frog, a process which I seem to remember took about three months in all.

This year I have found toadspawn, too, in the trough in our field, distinguishable from frogspawn by its eggs laid in ribbons of a jelly-like substance. Toads are good friends to any gardener, and in my garden there always seem to be a few around. As a single female lays about seven thousand eggs every year, it is perhaps surprising that it is not more common.

As I take a last look at the flowers by the river and make my way home, I think of Tennyson's lines:

'Now fades the last long streak of snow
Now burgeons every maze of quick
About the flowering squares, and thick
By ashen roots the violets blow.'

We will have to wait a few weeks for the quick – an old English name for hawthorn – to blossom, but in the meantime we have violets and primroses to enjoy; what in the world could be a simpler and more delightful pleasure?

Jack Higgins is man who knows his own mind, is used to getting his own way and is known up the dale as 'an ockard old bugger'.

Jack had come to see me over a year ago following a road traffic accident in which he had been involved, when a man had driven into the back of his car at some traffic lights. Jack had reacted in a predictable way and, after casting doubts on the other driver's parentage and asking him fairly crudely where he had learnt to drive, he called the police. His parting shot to the unfortunate motorist had been:

'It'll be to pay for, Ah tell thee, it will that.'

Apart from a few scratches and a fairly minor whiplash injury to his neck, Jack was unhurt, but it was clear from the first moment he consulted me that he was out to get as large a sum for damages as possible.

He had, according to his doctor, made a full recovery from his injuries within two months, and he instructed me to commence negotiations with the other driver's insurers. Based on a study of recent court cases, I reckoned that Jack was likely to obtain between £750 and £1,000, but that the award was likely to be nearer the lower figure. Following the usual tactics employed by insurance companies in these cases, the other driver's insurers made an initially low offer of £500 which, following further negotiations they subsequently increased to £650. Jack, who had been enraged by the initial offer, was no more pleased with the revised offer and told me in no uncertain terms to start court proceedings.

'Ah've 'ad enuff o' these games', he said, 'tell 'em Ah'll see 'em in 'ell afore Ah teks their offer.'

'You'll have to see them in court first', I replied.

I had duly commenced court proceedings, and the insurance company replied by admitting liability and paying into court the sum of £750. At that stage I had called Jack into my office.

'This is the moment of decision', I had said to him. 'If you accept £750 you will get it now and the insurers will be liable to pay your legal costs. If you don't accept it and the judge's award does not better £750, then you will have to pay the other side's costs as well as my firm's costs for going to court. It's a gamble, and I think you should consider accepting the payment into court very carefully indeed.'

'Nay, Mr Francis, Ah reckon t' job's worth at least a thousand an' tha's not tellin' me any different. Ah've med me mind up.'

'It's up to you, Mr Higgins, but you have been warned', I replied.

I had felt uneasy at Jack's attitude as we had waited for a trial date, and now at last this April day was to be the moment of truth. Would the judge's award beat the payment into court? We waited with baited breath as the judge, after having all the evidence and particularly the medical evidence, gave his decision. He awarded £775. The pay-in had been beaten by £25. It had been a close-run thing, but Jack had got his costs and I thought he would be delighted. Not a bit of it.

'Ah reckon that judge 'as nivver 'ad 'is neck in a bloody collar. It's disgustin' what 'e's given us', was Jack's response to the court judgment.

He stamped off out of court, muttering expletives as he made his way to the car park.

Some people never realise how lucky they are. I am beginning to see what they mean about Jack Higgins up the dale.

It is a rare season when apple, cherry, pear and plum are in blossom together. This year the plum blossom, virgin-white against the tree's bare branches, came early and was quickly turned to brown by late frosts. The pear and cherry are now in full bloom, and the apple, best of all with its delicate pink and white blossom, is yet to come.

Many blossoms are uncertain in their time of appearance – the may, for instance, often avoiding the month by which it is commonly called – but I can never remember a year when the cherry did not flower in April. Whenever I see the cherry blossom, I see in my mind's eye the garden of the old manor house where I lived as a boy. There was a fine old cherry tree growing next to an equally splendid silver birch tree.

The poet A E Housman described the cherry as 'loveliest of trees', and the silver birch has always been known as 'the queen of the forest'. Certainly these two trees made for a marvellous combination in my old garden, particularly in spring when they were all white and green and silver. But we children who feasted so royally from the other fruit trees never managed to pick any ripe cherries. The birds always beat us to them.

In his immortal lines from *A Shropshire Lad*, Housman told of his melancholy and despair that 'of his three score years and ten, twenty would not come again', and that 'another fifty years gave little room to look at things in bloom'. I suppose that the brief beautiful blossoming reminded him, as it must surely remind us all, that life itself is a fleeting and fragile as the cherry blossom, and that we should appreciate the natural world whilst we can.

When I look at the cherry blossom, I understand and feel the melancholy of the poet, but I strive to temper it with the philosophy of the gardener. There is after all, as we read in Eccleciastes, 'a time to be born, a time to die, a time to plant and a time to pluck up that which is planted'.

My gardening mentor 'Owd Jacob' had his own philosophy. I often remember the time we stood together in the orchard of my boyhood garden, watching the last of the cherry blossom blow away on an April breeze. Noticing the wistful look in my eyes, he put his large hands gently on my shoulders, and in a kind but reassuring voice he repeated a line from one of his favourite old popular songs:

'All be t' same in a hundred years, lad.'

Back to work, and accordingly back down to earth when I find myself advising on a shoplifting case. Such cases are often among the saddest and most difficult for solicitors, particularly when they concern, as so often they do, middle-aged ladies with no previous convictions who have led a hitherto unblemished life, but who also have medical, matrimonial or emotional problems - or a combination of all three.

The lady who was sitting in our reception waiting to see me did not look at all like the type of person one is accustomed to see facing a criminal charge. Muriel Smith was smartly dressed and her hair had obviously just been permed. I had no sooner closed the door of my office behind her when she burst into tears, and it was a good five minutes before she had sufficiently recovered to speak.

'I feel so ashamed, Mr Francis, I can hardly bear to think about it, let alone talk about it', she said, as she passed a summons across my desk.

She had been charged with stealing a tin of salmon from a city supermarket.

She told me all about her trip to the supermarket, where she had intended to buy a few items of food for herself. She hadn't been able to make up her mind exactly what she wanted, and had kept taking items off the shelves and then replacing them. When eventually she had made her selection – or thought she had - she paid for the items in her basket at the checkout and walked out of the store. Suddenly she had felt a tap on her shoulder, and a young woman who identified herself as a store detective had said to her:

'Excuse me, but I have reason to believe you have taken an item of food from the shop without paying for it. Would you please accompany me to the manager's office.'

In a voice which was by now reduced to a tremble, Muriel told how she had stood in the manager's office whilst waiting for the police. She had then been asked to remove her coat, and from one of the pockets the police officer produced a tin of salmon. She had gone pale, gasped, tried to speak but no words would come.

'I must have put it there without thinking', she had said at last. 'I had no idea – can I pay for it now?'

She went on to tell me of the humiliation of her subsequent arrest and of the statement she had made to the police under caution.

After I had taken down Muriel's statement of what had happened at the supermarket, I gently persuaded her to talk about her personal circumstances at the time of the alleged theft.

It transpired that she had been widowed only six months ago, and her loneliness and bereavement were made that much more difficult to bear because she had no children or close relatives to comfort her. She had been completely devoted to her husband, a non-smoking, teetotal, keep-fit fanatic who had died of a massive heart attack on a squash court at the age of fifty-one. She was herself menopausal, depressed, emotional and taking tranquilisers prescribed by her doctor.

'I just haven't been able to concentrate properly since Peter died. My mind wasn't working when I was in the supermarket', she explained to me, 'but I did take the tin of salmon without paying for it, so I must plead guilty. You see, Mr Francis, I've got very little money. My husband always reckoned he'd live to be a hundred so he didn't believe in life assurance. I'm afraid I may have to sell the house because I can't afford the mortgage.'

'You don't have to plead guilty, you know', I said to her, 'because it has to be proved not only that you took the tin of salmon without paying for it, but that you intended to steal it, and you didn't did you?'

'Certainly not', she replied.

'Well then, if you're going to plead not guilty – as I think you should – we'll have to decide whether the case should be heard by magistrates or by a Crown court jury.'

'Will a Crown court mean waiting a long time?', she asked, 'I don't think I could stand waiting. I just want to get the whole business over and done with.'

'It will mean waiting a bit longer, but isn't it important to give yourself the best possible chance of being aquitted? You see, magistrates have over the the years heard just about every excuse under the sun ever invented for shoplifting, whereas the members of a jury are more likely to be sympathetic and say to themselves: "There but for the grace of God go I".'

She thought for a while before replying.

'I'll take your advice, Mr Francis.'

To cut a long story short, we prepared Muriel's case for trial at the Crown court. Just before the hearing we had an unexpected piece of good fortune. Through the post – unsolicited and anonymous – came a copy of an internal memorandum within the supermarket organisation. Astonishingly, this memorandum from senior management expressed concern at the falling level of shoplifting, which indicated to management that the goods were not being sufficiently well displayed! Irrelevant to the facts of the case though this information undoubtedly was, I was determined that one way or another the jury would hear about it.

So when the supermarket manager came to give his evidence and was cross-examined, George Halton, the experienced barrister I had briefed to defend Muriel, flourished the memorandum in the air, read out the bits which mattered and asked:

'Does this memorandum represent your company's policy?'

The manager went red in the face and, as he attempted to bluster, the judge came to his rescue:

'What relevance does this document have to your client's case?', he asked George Halton.

George had to stop this line of questioning regarding the memorandum, but by this time it did not matter, for the jury now knew its contents.

The jury heard all the evidence, and in particular of the distressing personal circumstances of my client. The judge's summing up was very much biased towards the prosecution – sometimes in my experience a distinct advantage for the defence. He ended with this statement:

'Members of the jury, if you try this case with your hearts you will acquit, but you have to try the case with your heads.'

After a very short retirement the jury returned to give a not guilty decision. Muriel remained outwardly calm until we had left court, when she burst into floods of tears. In truth, the ordeal of appearing at court for ladies like her is a much greater punishment by far than any penalty which can be imposed by the court.

I went to see Muriel soon afterwards in her home. There she was, alone, surrounded by photos of her dead husband and living on her memories. I think, however, that she will survive like many ladies of her age who are similarly financially distressed, life-battered and making do alone and unsupported, but proudly independent and who bravely step out every day and say 'good morning' to the world.

Back at home, we have just acquired a great dane puppy and seven pet lambs. We really must be mad, but then I have always recognised that insanity is one of the chief qualifications for living in the country!

Rosemary and I have only owned three dogs the whole of our married life. The first, Flossie, an English pointer, was a wedding present and lived for fifteen years, a good age for any dog, particularly a pointer. She was loyal, affectionate, gentle, obedient and eminently biddable.

Our second dog Sally, an airedale terrier, shares the first three of Flossie's qualities but there the similarity ends, for she is totally ungovernable and cannot be let off the lead, not at any rate in our area which is sheep country. Airedales, a cross between otter hounds and terriers, are natural hunting dogs and once they get the scent they are off. In my painful experience, no power on earth can then recall them.

Sally is elderly now, but since Chloe the great dane puppy arrived she has taken on a new lease of life. Great danes are the gentle giants of the dog world, but they are extraordinarily large and clumsy. I have already tripped over her a few times, and as I write I have to keep a sharp eye on my manuscript. Puppies will, it seems, chew anything, particularly sheets of paper which they do not rate important!

As for the pet lambs, well, based on past experience, it will be a triumph if we manage to keep them all alive. We had a shock the very day they arrived. One of them swelled up in her tummy like a balloon, and Rosemary rushed her down to the local vet. She was agitated before she arrived there, and when she saw there was a lengthy queue her agitation and anxiety increased, for she reckoned that if she didn't see the vet immediately she would have one dead lamb on her hands. Sitting next to Rosemary in the waiting room was a grizzled old sheep farmer who had brought his dog with him. Glancing at the lamb and clearly puzzled by my wife's extreme anxiety, he said:

'Nay, there's no cause to fret, missus, it's nowt but a bit o' wind.'

The lamb survived, but I expect there will be more problems to come.

Knowing Rosemary, the lambs will all be given names. It is perhaps inevitable but will possibly be a mistake when the time comes, as surely it will, for them to go to market. 'Do they have to go?', asked one of our children the last time we reared pet lambs. I fear the answer had to be 'yes', because our field is not a large one and it will certainly not support too many geriatric sheep.

It is as well, in any case, that children should learn that the countryside is a workplace where there is dirt and death as well as beauty and balm, and where animals are bred, reared and killed.

Visitors to the Dales often do not realise that the beauty of the countryside is man-made, thanks in the main to generations of farmers and to the foresight as well as the self-interest of landowners who planted woods and preserved estates to serve their sporting interests. How many visitors realise, for instance, that the heather on the moors is only maintained by careful combination of grouse shooting and sheep grazing? Without them it would undoubtedly vanish, to be replaced by scrubland and above all by poisonous and fast-spreading bracken.

Lambs, like children, grow up too quickly, so we must make the most of the time just before bedtime when Rosemary and I go into the stable with our storm lantern to give them their last bottle feed of milk by hand, and afterwards when we watch their last frolics of the day, their skipping, playing and their funny little bleatings. As Rosemary is fond of saying, 'There is nothing quite like a lamb'.

To play in the first league tennis match of the season requires positive thinking. Such a match is invariably played during the last week of the month, when the weather is without fail uninviting. As I come down the steps of the village club house, I see a fisherman on the riverbank at the other side of the courts, and console myself with the thought that at least I am likely to be warmer that he is.

A good, long knock-up is what I need at the start of any tennis match, particularly when it is the first match of the season and I am woefully short of practice. It is a good job I have brought my old wooden racquet with me so that we can spin for choice of service or ends, for the modern metal racquets do not carry a 'rough or smooth' side. I once believed the day would never dawn when I would discard my faithful wooden racquet, but I discovered on trying the new and larger metal racquet that, once you have become accustomed to serving with it, the larger racquet head with its bigger 'sweet area' enables middle-aged players like myself to cover the net better, and is in all other respects a vast improvement.

After the knock-up, play begins rather nervously. My partner calls her opponent's forehand drive out. The call was correct, the ball landing a good six inches from the baseline. Our opponents looked disturbed by the call.

'How far was it out?', he called.

'Six inches', replied my partner.

'I'm not querying the call', he said (with neither of us really believing him). 'I just want to get my length.'

The first game goes to five deuces – doesn't it always? I am feeling weary and it is only the first game. Five sets and a good two hours of competitive tennis lie ahead.

Two hours later it is getting dark, and fortunately my partner and I win the last set 6-0.

As I leave the clubhouse after the usual after-match tea, I am already beginning to feel stiff, and I know very well that even after a hot bath and a good night's sleep I shall feel even stiffer in the morning. I feel better, though, and curiously elated. There is nothing like a spot of vigorous exercise for restoring the spirit when you are feeling tired or depressed.

It will continue to require positive thinking, but I hope there will be many more Aprils in years to come when I can play the first tennis match of the season, for the month would not be quite the same for me without it.

Chapter Five

'But the merriest month in all the year
Is the merry month of May.'
    Robin Hood and the Three Squires

Arncliffe and Appletreewick, Dacre and Darley, Sawley and Summer-bridge, Fellbeck and Fountains Earth. The names of many of our Dales villages trip off the tongue like poetry, particularly when you are travelling around countryside which displays all the freshness and loveliness of early May. It always seems such a crying shame to have to work in an office on such a day, but I know very well that come some bitterly cold and wet day next winter when I see a gang of workmen labouring at the roadside, I would not exchange my place in a dry, warm, centrally-heated office for theirs.

Maypole dancing and morris dancing are the proper traditional English ways to celebrate the time of year. The local schoolchildren have already greeted the month as they have done for generations past by dancing around the maypole and by crowning their May queen, and last weekend the high street was packed with people to see some visiting morris dancers perform, adding their unique colour, pageant and tradition to the daily life of the dale.

Before setting off in my car this morning, I had time for a quick walk around my garden, which in early May is what I have always described as being at the 'inbetween stage'. The rockeries are past their best, the roses and herbaceous borders are yet to come.

In nature's garden which lies in the countryside beyond, however, it is a different story. The woods carpeted with bluebells appear from a distance to have a ground cover of blue mist, whilst in damp meadows adjoining the woods the lady's smock is in flower.

Country people have often called these flowers 'milkmaids' or 'cuckoo flowers', the latter presumably because their season was thought to coincide with the calling of the cuckoo. Shakespeare memorably described lady's smocks as 'painting the meadows with delight', which indeed they do, particularly when there are orange tip butterflies, with their delicate mottled green undersides, fluttering among them. Happily where there are lady's smocks there are likely to be orange tips, because they, along with jack-by-the-hedge, are the butterfly's principal food plants.

I still feel the same sense of excitement and pleasure at seeing the first orange tip butterfly of the year as I did as a butterfly-collecting schoolboy, for it is surely one of the prettiest of our native species.

I am delighted anew by the fresh green of the fields, trees and hedgerows. The sycamore, birch and alder trees by the river are fully in leaf, and in our garden, which is a little higher up, the last two trees to foliate are the mountain ash and the copper beech. The last is a particulary fine specimen, probably planted in Victorian times when our house was built.

It is fascinating to watch the copper beech come into leaf – at first, light in colour, and then after only a few days, a rich dark shade of copper. Only the mountain ash is yet to come out. If the oak comes before the ash then we're only supposed to get a splash, but in our part of the world at any rate I have never known a season when the oaks did not come into leaf first.

The dale has taken on that pastoral hue which it always does for a few precious weeks every summer, the cuckoo is calling somewhere, the bees are humming among the sycamores and the catoneasters, and the swallows are back. There are, however, other matters for a solicitor even on a morning like this, and it was time for me to go to work.

My 'matter for a May morning' when I arrived at the office was an appointment with Martha Stringcliffe's nephew, James Ackroyd. I was saddened to learn that his aunt had died the previous day.

I had known Martha since I was a boy, when she had taken an interest in me for the sole reason that she was a famed local poultry keeper and she knew that I kept a few hens myself. I shall always be grateful to her for teaching me just about everything I ever knew about poultry keeping, from the best feeding methods to the price I should charge my mother for the eggs laid by my hens.

Martha was always quite unlike most of the small poultry keepers I knew, whose hen runs typically consisted of a series of ramshackle old huts surrounded by a small area of sour, rock-hard soil pitted with hollows, containing discarded pieces of scrap metal, clumps of nettles and bounded by rusty, broken-down wire netting. Martha's poultry were always kept immaculately in 'five star' hen houses, and she kept at least two separate outside runs which she regularly limed so that neither became sour nor over-used. Her hens were always well fed and scrupulously cleaned. With their bright red combs, they always looked the picture of health.

Whenever I think of Martha, I see her in my mind's eye, mashing up boiled potato peelings for the morning feed and then going out to her hens, eyeing them and then saying to me:

'Now John, that's what hens should look like. You'll never see battery hens looking like that, poor things.'

Now Martha had never married, and as she became older so she also became an increasingly eccentric recluse. More and more she shunned human company, and was only truly happy and contented when she was among her hens. She always kept rhode island reds (which she called 'my rhodies'), together with a dozen brown leghorns, half a dozen morans for their rich speckledy-brown eggs, and a few handsome but rather elderly bantams. Together they were her pride and joy, her consolation and her life.

The cottage she had lived in all her life was, by way of contrast to her hen houses, tumbledown and chaotically untidy. She had received a number of visits from social workers at the behest of anxious relatives and neighbours, but had indignantly sent them all packing.

'I'm perfectly alright here with my hens – I'm not moving for you or for anyone', she had told them.

James told me that she had died suddenly the previous day whilst throwing corn pellets to her beloved hens and watching them scratching for them. Some little time before her death, Martha had made a will with me, and I was able to remember its terms as they were rather unusual. I now addressed myself to her nephew.

'I'm extremely sorry to hear about your aunt, James. You know that you and I are her executors, I expect. Presumably you've already made the funeral arrangements.'

'I've done more than that, Mr Francis', replied James, a business executive who had little time for his aunt's lifestyle and had tried in vain for years to tidy her up. 'I felt I just had to do something straight away about those old hens and bantams. I've done what Martha should have done years ago. There's a man who's always advertising in the local paper for old hens or other unwanted stock.

Well I rang him straight away, and he was delighted for a few quid to take them all away to the knacker's yard for hens or whatever it's called. You'll be pleased I've got one problem solved, I expect.'

I had listened with increasing concern.

'Did your aunt never tell you the terms of her will?', I asked him.

'No, she never liked talking about it', he replied.

'Well, in that case I had better tell you now that you and I, as her executors, are required by the will to set aside sufficient funds from her estate to provide for the maintenance and feeding of all her surviving hens and bantams for the rest of their lives.'

James' face was a picture of disbelief and horror as he realised what he had done.

'What do we do now?', he asked me eventually.

I gave him the lawyer's answer.

'I think I need notice of that question – but it's going to be a bit difficult now, wouldn't you say?'

Rosemary and I have managed to take a few days' holiday this month, and our destination has been the magical island of Mull in the Hebrides, which we discovered for the first time six years ago.

It generally rains on the west coast of Scotland, so we packed our anoraks and gumboots, and were well prepared if it turned out wet.

The cares of the world disappeared, just as they did six years ago under the spell of the island's magic. The holiday was once again a re-enactment of our childhood and of childhood literature, for on Mull we found *Swallows and Amazons*, a *Famous Five* adventure and *Treasure Island* all rolled into one. We were children again.

The precious few days have been and gone, but what happy and lingering memories they hold; of seeing a red squirrel on the journey through Perthshire, the first since I was a boy; of a boat trip to Staffa, Mendelssohn's island, where Rosemary descended into Fingal's Cave down a slippery path by a rockface overlooking the sea like an experienced commando, a route which I faced rather less bravely; of watching puffins, seals, and deer; and of Carsaig, where on an enchanting walk in woods full of primroses and bluebells, we saw on the hills above a herd of wild goats, descendants of the domesticated herds which roamed the mountains prior to the Highland clearances. I had particularly wanted to make a sentimental journey to Carsaig, for the lonely telephone kiosk there was the setting for a scene in one of my favourite films, *I Know Where I'm Going*. How very sad to see that, even in the Hebrides, the distinctive British red telephone kiosks are being systematically replaced by their appalling functional all glass and yellow successors.

Memories, too, of walking and sightseeing and exploring; of swimming in Calgary Bay, with only oystercatchers for company, where the sea seemed even colder than it was in Norway where I once swam in a fjord under snow-capped mountains; of ceilidhs and dances; of a visit to Iona, and a walk across the island to an unspoilt bay to the accompaniment of the sound of seabirds and skylarks, where the waves splashed onto a beach of silver-white sand over smooth, brilliantly coloured pebbles. We sat together on a thrift-covered outcrop, looking out over a sea which could only be described as Hebridean blue, a welcome contrast to much of our coastline where the colour of the sea is more a dirty brown. Hebridean colours are vibrant and almost translucent.

The only thing I regretted as we took the small ferry to Lochaline and left Mull behind was that I did not take my fishing rod with me, for I was sorely tempted every time we passed a loch, river or burn. However, a few days away together should, I think, be spent together. Rosemary does not fish, and fishing – like writing – is a solitary and unsociable occupation.

It is surprising how quickly the memory of a holiday fades once you are back at work, but whenever in the future I am in a traffic jam, at a cocktail party in a room full of people, the phone is ringing incessantly and office life is fraught, or when I am otherwise caught up in the rush, bustle and tumult of life in the late twentieth century, I shall think of the serenity, peace and tranquility of Mull, where eagles soar above her lofty mountains.

I always find it hard going at the office after a holiday, but my despair at the sight of a desk full of files and correspondence is tempered by my delight in being among my own people again.

One of the pleasures of practising law in a small Dales market town like Denley, where I have spent most of my working life, is that it is impossible for me to walk along the high street without meeting friends and clients – but it can be a problem too.

On my very first day back at work, I had to pop out of the office to see my bank manager. I fully intended to be away for only a few minutes, but no sooner had I emerged into the street when who should

I see coming towards me but 'Lucky Jim' Bottomley. There was no avoiding him.

'Ah've jus' cum straight frae t' doctors, Mr Francis, an' it looks like it'll be a reight long job.'

'What will be a long job?', I asked rather tersely.

'Why, me backache of course. Surely tha's not forgotten? Ah were tellin' thee about it ovver at t' market last Monday.'

As he spoke, I did remember our conversation all too well – for it was more of a monologue. At this moment I was trying desperately to think of an excuse to avoid having to listen to his story yet again.

'Well, it's like this yer see . . . '

As Jim launched into his story again, I noticed brothers Fred and Joe Westgate walking along the other side of the road past the Denley Heifer public house. At last, my chance to catch them both together had come – or so I thought.

'I'm sorry, Mr Bottomley, you'll have to excuse me. I've just seen some people I must talk to.'

As I dashed away to cross the road with Jim still trying to tell me about his back problem, I saw Fred and Joe glance in my direction. At the same time, it seemed to me that the brothers' walking pace suddenly increased. By the time I had crossed the road, Fred and Joe were fifty yards away, and as soon as they turned into the crowded market place I knew that I had lost them. At that moment I remembered in my frustration the words of my secretary Clare:

'That'll be the day when you catch those two together.'

I retraced my steps, and as I passed the bus shelter I smiled to myself, for it reminded me of a story told about Cyril Boothroyd, the old senior partner in my firm of Boothroyd and Lytton, who was still practising law when I started there as a very raw articled clerk.

Cyril was very upright and proper, a gentleman solicitor of the old school. He never learnt to drive, and went everywhere by bus or taxi.

The story goes that one day he was waiting in the shelter for his bus. There was also a young couple, engaging in the sort of behaviour one tends to associate with young couples in bus shelters.

After watching their horse play for some minutes and listening to their 'oohs' and 'aahs' and squeals, Cyril walked slowly over to them and said to the girl, very seriously and very deliberately.

'Are you being molested, my dear?'

'Yes, thank you', she pertly replied.

64

As I passed the supermarket next door to my bank, who should I see but my old friends George and Elinor Dixon loading their groceries into their car – including a bottle of whisky.

As I approached them from behind, I couldn't resist the opportunity of surprising them.

'Is that for cousin Joseph?', I asked, pointing at the bottle.

'Oh, it's only you Mr Francis', said George, as he turned round and recognised me to his obvious relief. 'An there Ah were, frettin' missen that there were someone else who were in on t' little secret of ours', he added with a broad smile and a knowing wink.

My business at the bank did not keep me there long. When I came out and passed the supermarket again, I saw Fred Hellifield sitting in his car at the edge of the car park.

'I bet he's given the shopping orders to his wife Mary and is bossing her around as usual', I thought to myself.

My thoughts were immediately confirmed when I saw Mary staggering to the car with a load of provisions. I could just hear what Fred was saying, as he sat in state and offered her no help:

'Wheer 'ave you bin, woman? Ah've gitten sum work to do back at t' farm, an' Ah can't stop 'ere all day, tha knows.'

I was still shaking my head as I made my way back to the office. 'Lucky Jim' was still in the street outside, but I was relieved to see that this time he was talking to local estate agent Dick East. From the exasperated expression on Dick's face, he was not enjoying the experience.

I just caught a few words as I hurried past and retreated into the safety of my office.

'Ah reckoned they'd fettled me back reight enuff ovver at t' hospital, like, but *un*fortunately . . . '

If just after Christmas is the busy time for divorce work in the office, then spring and early summer is very definitely the probate season.

I seem to be spending a lot of time this month doing my best to comfort widows and to help them administer their late husband's estates as smoothly as possible. It is widows rather than widowers in nine cases out of ten. Women still generally live longer than men, so it is they who as a rule have to adapt to being alone and carrying on life somehow. It is as well, perhaps, for I have noticed that they seem better able to do so than men.

Death has seemingly replaced sex as the taboo subject and the one topic which people are reluctant to confront or discuss. I have noticed that there is also a general inability to know how to talk to the bereaved. How many times have I heard folk say after meeting a recently bereaved friend in town:

'It's so sad, I just didn't know what to say.'

I have found as a solicitor that it helps widows if they can find somebody to talk to about their late husband. They usually want to describe the last moments of their loved ones' lives, their hospital treatment in detail, and then to go back further and recount the happy experiences of a long married life. I do not think anyone should feel embarrassed or attempt to cut short these reminiscences, for they are, I feel sure, a part of the grieving process and a necessary step in progress back to normality. I often recall Swinburne's lines:

'And time remembered is grief forgotten
and frosts slain and flowers begotten.'

I have noticed two other facets of death. The first is that sudden death, particularly in a young person, is harder to bear than death following a long illness; and the second is that the rich generally find death harder to come to terms with than the poor. They discover very quickly that there is no comfort in a luxurious home, in wall-to-wall carpeting, or in expensive fixtures and fittings.

I have observed, too, that people's reactions to death vary. Some cry a lot, some are business-like, others put on a brave face and hide their true feelings, but they all need company, comfort and time. In the midst of the busy lives most people lead these days, too few of them seem to have the time or be prepared to make the time to listen anymore.

The extended family has for the most part gone, people do not turn automatically to their parish priest as used to be the case, and perhaps there is not the same comfort to be found in a medical centre as used to be found in a family doctor. The result is that the lawyer dealing with the estate is often the only person available for the bereaved to talk to.

There is something particularly poignant in cases where someone has died and has outlived all his or her friends. On one occasion I arranged a funeral where I was the only person there. Undertakers tell me that this happens quite frequently. How terribly sad to leave this world without the support and presence of a single friend.

As I press on with my files in the office and contemplate the sad circumstances of my bereaved clients, I often reflect that for a solicitor there should always be more to probate work than simply completing forms and preparing estate accounts.

One of the many hazards of being a solicitor is that there are always some people around who seem to think that they are entitled to free advice. This particular hazard can present itself at any time, but I have been reminded of it because twice already this month I have been approached like this at social occasions. It is not surprising therefore that solicitors, like doctors, strive to keep their profession secret when attending social or sporting functions.

I learnt this lesson some years ago when I was staying at a small hotel. One of the guests, whom I had foolishly told I was a solicitor, cornered me in the lounge after dinner whilst coffee was being served, and sought my advice upon an alleged injustice which he had suffered in a county court case some years previously. Before I knew what was happening, all the other guests had surrounded me, and I found myself in the centre of a circle of people all anxious to put their own particular legal question to me.

It seems to be an unhappy fact of life that most people have a 'hard luck story' to tell about their experiences with the law. These often arise from a will or the administration of an estate where they consider they have been cheated out of their due inheritance, or because they have been found guilty of a road traffic offence arising out of an accident for which they could not possibly have been responsible, or because they have been victims of what they consider to have been a complete miscarriage of justice.

I know of several solicitors who have developed their own particular technique when approached by someone at a cocktail party for 'free' advice about uncle Joe's estate or whatever. One I know always immediately presents his card on such occasions and says:

'I shall be delighted to discuss this matter with you if you will telephone my secretary at the office tomorrow and make an appointment to see me.'

Another lawyer of my acquaintance is much blunter. He always says to any cricket or golf-playing friend, who approaches him for advice on the assumption that it will be free:

'Now look lad, you realise you're into fees now?'

I have given my share of free advice over the years, but I hardly think the public can expect this facility to be provided in the future by the younger, more commercially-minded generation of lawyers. Come to think of it, why on earth should they? There is after all no such thing in this life as a free lunch, nor an automatic entitlement to free ale.

I have recently been reading a most interesting book written by Mr Alexander Pearson over forty years ago about his 'doings as a country solicitor' in the delightful town of Kirkby Lonsdale. He tells of the time he was advised to take up shooting, but was firmly warned:

'Clients who are hosts to a solicitor do not expect to have to pay for consultations which take place at their shooting parties.'

Plus ca change, plus c'est la même chose.

Retired schoolmaster Edward Naylor called in to see me one day this month to enquire whether he could obtain any compensation for injuries he had received after being mugged on his way home from his local pub one evening a few months ago. As he was walking the short distance to his house, he had suddenly and without any warning or explanation been set upon by two youths, punched about his face and body, forced to the ground and viciously kicked. His wallet which contained only £10 had been stolen, along with his cheque card, driving documents and, most sadly for him, several old photographs of his late wife which had been taken during their courting days just after the war. Edward's wife had died of cancer several years previously, and I knew that since then he had been living alone in a small flat, into which he had reluctantly moved after his wife's death.

He told me that following enquiries made at the pub, the police discovered that two youths matching Edward's description had been seen there drinking heavily during the evening, and had been observed following him when he left. They were subsequently arrested, charged and convicted of assault and robbery. One was placed on probation and the other received a community service order. Both were unemployed and no compensation order was made.

All this had happened over a period of six months, and now Edward had called on me to express his disgust at the apparent light sentences which had been imposed on his attackers, and to see whether there were any further steps which he could take. I immediately advised him to complete an application to the Criminal Injuries Compensation Board, a Government-funded body set up some years ago to compensate victims of crimes of violence. I duly helped Edward to complete the form, and now we shall have to wait many months for the board to complete its enquiries and determine what award if any should be made.

My fear is that, by the time the award is made, Edward may not be around to benefit from it. He was a sad, lonely man before he was mugged, but now he is a broken man. It makes me angry to look at the photographs of his injured face and body taken after the assault. His physical injuries will probably heal, but whether the mental scar arising from the mugging will ever disappear is, I think, extremely doubtful.

Some years ago, I played a small part in the formation of a victim support scheme in Denley. It seemed to me then, as it does now, that whereas the criminal – quite properly – receives a full range of assistance from the State, from legal aid to social services to probation after care, the victim frequently receives no help and is forgotten. I have therefore put Edward in touch with his local victim support scheme, in the hope that he will benefit from the company, comfort and advice which their volunteers are able to provide.

It is a sobering but true fact that the victims of crime often serve a life sentence, but criminals rarely do. When I think of Edward Naylor, a man who devoted his life to teaching generations of children and who has given freely of his time in service to his local community, it seems to me that when such a man falls victim to a crime of violence, he should at least be entitled to the same consideration and attention from society as those who have perpetrated the crime.

A solicitor's files will always contain many sad and serious cases like Edward's, but there are fortunately always a few which provide some light relief.

Some of the best examples of humour in the office are to be found in correspondence between solicitors, for even the most deadly serious exchange of letters can have its lighter moments.

For the last couple of months I have been acting on behalf of Ted and Josie Peart in their purchase of a small village house. As they are both exceptionally keen gardeners, they had asked me to make sure that all the garden plants and shrubs were included in the purchase price.

I subsequently wrote to the seller's solicitors, and amongst other questions relating to the property I asked the following one specifically:

'Would you please confirm that all the garden plants and shrubs are included in the agreed purchase price.'

Two days ago I received this reply:

'My clients confirm that all the garden plants and shrubs will be left, with the exception of the gooseberry bush which they wish to keep – for sentimental reasons.'

I was rather tickled by this reply and immediately telephoned the seller's solicitors.

'I never did believe that old story about the gooseberry bush – until I got your letter today', I said, still with a smile on my face.

These days, solicitors are more and more frequently consulted on what may be termed 'consumer problems'. I was reminded of this one day this month, when a young lady called Julia Mason came in to see me at my office in a state of some distress. The reason for her condition, as she immediately told me, was that earlier in the day she had discovered in a bottle of orange juice, from which she was about to pour herself a glass, what appeared to be the remnants of a long-dead bluebottle.

Now I have forgotten much of the law I learnt as a student, but just as most people remember the Battle of Hastings and *Magna Carta* from their history lessons at school, so nearly every lawyer remembers from his student days the celebrated case of *Donoghue v Stevenson*.

In that case, a certain young lady had gone with a friend to a cafe in Paisley. There the friend bought for her a large bottle of ginger beer. The cafe proprietor then poured some of the contents of the bottle into a glass and she drank it. When her friend emptied the rest of the bottle into the glass, out floated the decomposed remains of a snail before her very eyes. This sad mishap caused the good lady to suffer from both shock and gastro-enteritis. When she had recovered, she sued the manufacturer of the ginger beer. The House of Lords made the historic decision that, on the facts, the manufacturer owed her a 'duty of care'; however, their lordships gave their opinion that there was not enough evidence for them to decide whether the manufacturers had been negligent in permittting the snail to select such an unusual grave!

I told Julia all about *Donoghue v Stevenson* and its relevance to her own case, and advised her that, apart from any criminal charges which might be brought against the seller by the public health authorities, she might very well have a claim for compensation herself if scientific analysis backed her up.

Reflecting upon the case after Julia had left, it occurred to me that, in years gone by, people would not have even thought about consulting a lawyer in such a case. We are as a society becoming more litigation-minded, following the trend established in America and now reaching absurd proportions there. People do not now say, as they used to, when something goes wrong, 'It's an accident' or 'It's one of those things'. They look instead for somebody to blame. Like Mrs Ramsbottom in the story of *Albert and the Lion*, they are wont to say:

'Someone's got to be summonsed.'

I doubt whether this is a healthy trend in society. In any case, how on earth do you assess appropriate damages for the shock of discovering a decomposed fly in a glass of orange?

Chapter Six

'*A noise like of a hidden brook.*
In the leafy month of June,
That to the sleeping woods all night
Singeth a quiet tune.'
        Samuel Taylor Coleridge

The shyness of spring and early summer has given away to the luxurious and wanton growth which I shall always associate with midsummer.

The mauve flowers of the lilac tree beside the summerhouse are gone, but when they were in full bloom last month, they reminded me of English country lanes and Ivor Novello. Beneath it are a few foxgloves, and in a weedier, more remote part of the garden there are many more examples of this magical and medicinal flower.

Truly the foxglove is a flower for the wild garden. Traditionally associated with foxes or fairies, I am not altogether sure where the origin of the name lies, but I prefer to believe that once upon a time it was the flower of the little folk, that in old English it was called 'the folk's glove' which was translated in country speech to foxglove. At all events, whenever I look at foxgloves I am transported in my mind to some distant and magical garden of childhood where I am trying to fit the petals of the flowers over a grubby fingernail, being wary of a pollen-covered bumble bee at the very base of the flower, and thinking about the story of Little Grey Rabbit and the weasels, whose den was camouflaged by the flowers.

In the more formal part of the garden, the first roses are in flower, the bedding-out plants are establishing themselves and, in the mixed border, lupins, geums and campanulas are all competing with one another in a riot of colour. Beside our front gate, an elderberry tree is in full bloom, reminding me of a summer years ago when we made champagne from the flowers, which not surprisingly the children rated better than lemonade. I have, too, a less happy memory of the time we made elderberry cordial, and in the following winter the bottles exploded one by one and we were continually clearing up the sticky purple liquid.

Up on Silver Hill the wild flowers are at their best. The verges, which mercifully the council leaves alone these days, are full of vetches, birdsfoot trefoil, speedwell and abundant cow parsley, which is now waist high.

Back in the house, Melanie, who is in the middle of taking her A-levels, is playing the piano to relieve her tension. Among her many talents is an ability to play any tune by ear. I envy her this, for I am undoubtedly the least musical member of the family. This melancholy fact does not, however, prevent me from singing at the top of my voice in the bath, when I imagine myself taking bows following innumerable encores at some famous concert hall. 'Vanity of vanities', sayeth the preacher, 'all is vanity'.

It is a Sunday evening and, as I contemplate the colourful and pastoral scene in the garden and up the dale beyond, I shudder as I think about the week which lies ahead. There are two evening meetings to attend which are associated with local societies; I am to give a lunchtime talk to Denley Rotary Club; there are two tennis matches to play if the weather holds; there is a church function; there are umpteen jobs to do in the garden; and there are family commitments. At the office my indispensable secretary Clare is away, I am already two weeks behind with my work, I have three court cases to prepare, I have a full diary of appointments, and there is drafting and paperwork which has already been left too long. Ah well, as Major Bunn, my old tennis mentor and Classics scholar, was fond of saying:

'Pro bono publico, no bloody panico!'

June is no different to any other month in that, being a country solicitor, I have to spend a lot of time inspecting properties which my clients are buying and selling. In the city or the suburbs, solicitors can usually identify the terraced or semi-detached house quite easily from plans on title deeds. Where I practise law, it is by no means that simple. It is not just the descriptions of the properties which are sometimes difficult to follow, it is that there are other important matters which need careful investigation, like boundaries, septic tanks, shared driveways and rights of way.

Early this week I found myself reading a description of a property which was stated to be 'bounded on the north by a dry stone hedge now or formerly belonging to Albert Smith'. I smiled as I read this, because although there are countless dry stone walls in the Dales, I have not yet come across a dry stone hedge; so if Albert Smith, whoever he was, possessed one in days of yore he must have been unique!

Very often there is no plan at all with title deeds and, unless you have the very long and accurate memory of a local property owner, a description to the effect that 'the property is bounded by land now or formerly owned by Joe Bloggs' is of little value.

If there is a plan with the deeds, you are not necessarily much better off. Only last week I was standing in the middle of an old higgledy-piggledy property in Denley, trying desperately to relate the plan to what I was actually looking at. The plan was annexed to a conveyance made in 1879, and of course there had been many physical changes to the property since then. The ashes pit and outside privy shown on the plan were nowhere to be seen, and part of the building had clearly been extended. There was another small building shown on the plan which I could not identify. I pointed out the difficulty to my client, who then tried to use his local knowledge to help me.

'Ah well, that were wheer t' auld mistal were once ovver', he explained as he looked over my shoulder at the plan.

This reminded me of the tale about the traveller who sought directions to a certain house from an old Dalesman he met in a village.

'Reight, lad. Well, tha carries on down t' road, an' then tha teks t' fust left about a mile an' a quarter past t' old house that were burnt down to t' ground twenty year sin.'

I was reflecting as I returned to the office that ashes pits, outbuildings and privies

– particularly the latter – are a snare and a delusion for the unwary solicitor. In my early days as a very raw assistant solicitor, I once conveyed a row of back-to-back terraced houses and completely failed to include the outside lavatories which went with them, an omission which could have seriously 'inconvenienced' my clients!

It never ceases to amaze me to what lengths and to what expense some people are prepared to go in matters which to the outsider appear trivial and not worth the trouble.

Some years ago, I appeared in a county court case on behalf of a lady who was suing a furniture upholsterer about a lounge chair which she said had not been repaired correctly. The upholsterer defended the action, and both parties called expert witnesses in support of their case. The county court registrar was obviously in some difficulty in weighing up the respective merits of what was obviously a highly technical matter, and eventually he said:

'I think that before coming to any decision in this case it is essential that I should inspect the chair in question.'

Now this lady lived in a remote village some distance from the court, so what followed was the rather strange spectacle of a number of cars containing the litigants, their solicitors, their witnesses, court officials and finally the county court registrar solemnly driving in procession down winding and seemingly endless country lanes for the sole purpose of inspecting a lounge chair.

This month I have again been reminded of some of the more bizarre aspects of litigation, and of the trivialities over which some people are apparently prepared to fight to the bitter end.

Earlier in the month, a farmer client of mine called Robin Jackson was about to sign a contract to buy a farm for just short of £500,000. The transaction nearly fell through because he and the seller quarrelled over whether the brass door knocker to the farmhouse was included in the price. In desperation, the estate agent who had negotiated the sale offered to buy a new one himself – I dare say he would have bought a dozen if it had secured the sale and his commission – but Robin was adamant:

'Nay, it's t' one that's already theer Ah wants – nowt else 'll do.'

Eventually, and with much ill-will, the seller gave way, and a rather soured transaction went through – but it had been a mighty close-run thing.

Husbands and wives often quarrel, when their marriages break down, over the division of household contents. In the absence of any agreement, such disputes have to be resolved in court. Can there be any more ludicrous sight, I have often thought, than that of a county court registrar solemnly dividing up cups and saucers!

I had thought I was going to avoid this prospect in Jean's case, for she had told me that she and husband Mark had settled everything between them when they separated last month.

Yesterday, however, I received a letter from Mark's solicitors which read:

'Kindly ask your client to arrange for the immediate return to our client of the following personal items – one jockstrap, a length of rope, his carving knife, the large hammer and a pair of pliers.'

My imagination ran riot as I contemplated that particular combination!

Just this last week in another matrimonial case, the parties were able to agree to a division of the household contents with just one exception. There were two sets of blankets, one pink and the other blue; both husband and wife insisted on having the blue blankets. This crucial matter looked to be all set for a court hearing, when I managed to resolve it by making a very non-legal suggestion to the wife's solicitor:

'Why don't they just toss a coin to decide?'

They agreed, a mutual friend spun the coin, and I am extremely thankful to say my client called correctly.

'How on earth do you calculate a charge for advice like that?', I wondered afterwards.

In another case this month, following the death of their widowed mother, her two daughters, who were to share her estate but who had never got on well together, started taking various ornaments and pieces of furniture from her house. They then quarrelled violently, each claiming that the other had taken more than her fair share. As sole executor of the estate, I decided that there was only one course of action to be taken. I called them both in to my office.

'If you cannot agree a division of the household contents between you', I said, 'then I shall instruct a valuer to prepare an inventory. This will be expensive because he will have to inspect the complete contents. The contents will then have to be sold in their entirety.'

The daughters failed to agree, and it was perhaps poetic justice that, after the expenses of valuer, carrier and auctioneer, there was practically nothing left for them to share. Solicitors perhaps more that most people see many examples of 'cutting off noses to spite faces'.

This month has seen my younger son Johnny confirmed as a member of the Church of England. I was born an Anglican and an Anglican I will surely die, even in the face of all my doubts, concerns and misgivings about this national institution, as well as my love for it.

For the Church of England is a very curious mixture indeed. It owes its origins to an unseemly quarrel between an English king and an Italian pope; it is steeped in the history of our people; it is weighed down by a bureaucratic administration, an extensive portfolio of property and a burdensome responsibility to maintain a large number of buildings, whose architectural styles range from the sublime to the ridiculous; its services range from the 'bells and smells' of the Anglo-Catholic wing right through to its evangelical wing, and includes on its fringes the singing, clapping and dancing of the Charismatic movement so different from the hushed church atmosphere of my boyhood. Many of its new-style services contain the most banal English it is possible to conceive, and I miss the lovely language of the old services, particularly those most beautiful and comforting words: 'The peace of God which passeth all understanding'.

The Church finds it difficult to make up its collective mind on the burning issues of the day; it appoints bishops who appear to fancy themselves more as politicians than theologians; its doctrine appears muddled and confused; it will not remarry divorcees but will bless their marriages; it will baptise children whose parents request it for social reasons; and it cannot make up its mind whether or not to admit women to the priesthood. People no longer go to church very much, but yet they expect it always to be there.

The Church of England is an institution which defies all logic, yet for all its undoubted faults and contradictions I remain a staunch Anglican. It is, I think, partly because of the debt of knowledge I owe to all those Victorian parsons who wrote such marvellous books about birds, butterflies and flowers, and partly because of the comforting fact that it remains so essentially English in character, broadly based, tolerant and always seeking the middle ground. Its doors are always open and anyone may enter.

As I was talking to Johnny about my own faith and about his forthcoming confirmation, I was trying very hard to remember what I had learned from the many classes I attended which were presided over by my school chaplain. I am slightly ashamed to confess that the only thing I can now remember is the warning he gave to us that, in taking communion wine for the first time, we should not expect a particularly good vintage!

For all my doubts, reservations and criticisms of the Church of England and my own rather weak witness to its faith, I am glad that now all three of our children are confirmed members. I have at one time or another read about most of the world's great religions, but in choosing to remain an Anglican I can only echo the memorable words of Martin Luther:

'Here I stand, I can do no other.'

It is amazing how many people trip over holes in the road or uneven pavements at about eleven o'clock at night.

'Lucky Jim' was back in the office earlier this month, instructing me to claim damages for him because of just such an accident. He had been making his way home after an evening at Denley Social Club, when he had tripped over an unmarked 'hole' in a side street. The 'hole' lay about nine inches from the pavement and he had fallen full length, badly cutting and bruising himself, and twisting his ankle as he ended up sprawled over the ground.

'Lucky Jim' cut a sorry figure when he called in to see me a couple of days later. He hobbled into the office with the help of a stick. He had cuts and bruises all over his face, and he sported a fine pair of 'shiners'. He looked to all the world as if he had just emerged from a world championship fight, and I was hard put not to smile.

'Now then, Mr Bottomley, you look as if you've been in the wars', I said.

'It's a bloody disgrace', he replied. 'T' council's neglected t' road for years, but they'll not git away wi' this little lot', he continued, pointing to his disfigured face and his sprained ankle.

I took down details of his claim and wrote off to his doctor for a medical report. Jim had not broken anything, it was just a case of cuts, bruises, a sprained ankle and shock, so it would not be a substantial claim.

I went down to the scene of the accident. Sure enough there was a hole in the road, but I noticed that it was situated right underneath a street lamp and there was no reason why he should not have seen it. In any case, the 'hole' was barely three-quarters of an inch deep, and I was conscious of a sentence from the judgment in a leading case on 'trips':

'There may be a ridge of half an inch or three-quarters of an inch occasionally, but that is not the sort of thing which makes it dangerous or not reasonably safe.'

I reckoned that the local council would quote this case at me, but there was nothing to lose by submitting Jim's claim; which I did, accompanied by a copy of the medical report.

The council wrote back to say that, having inspected the scene of the accident, having measured the hole and having considered all the available evidence, they had decided not to make an offer. Now the council was under no obligation to disclose to me what evidence they had collected, but they later told me on the telephone that they had received no less than six unsolicited statements from witnesses, all saying that Jim had emerged from the club onto the street completely drunk, and that he had fallen in the road no fewer than three times before his final trip in the 'hole'.

I had to advise Jim that if he took the matter to court – and it was extremely doubtful whether the size either of the hole or the claim would justify it – he would have to face the fact that evidence of his drunkenness would be given, and the court would be asked to conclude that he had been the author of his own misfortune.

'T' judge'll nivver believe Jim Bottomley were drunk', said Jim, none too convincingly. 'But is it reight what tha tells me last time about t' 'ole bein' too small for t' law to reckon wi'? If that's t' case, Ah thinks we'd best forget t' job.'

Whatever Jim's real reasons were for withdrawing his claim, he had been thwarted again – and not for the first time this year.

One of my favourite radio comedians was the late Eric Barker. I particularly remember him for his famous double act with Deryck Guyler, when they played the parts of two old codgers sitting in a shelter on the sea front or in the lounge of some provincial hotel, holding rambling conversations on such English subjects as the weather and the difficulties of getting a good night's sleep.

I was reminded of their act when I recently went to see George and Albert Wrightson, two elderly brothers who farm a smallholding up the dale. They have been favourite clients of mine for many years, but the problem has always been to keep them to the subject in hand.

Now George is a sheep man through and through, and his sole criterion for judging his fellow human beings is whether or not they 'ken sheep', and whether they are able to hold a knowledgeable conversation about them. So if you do not know the difference between Dalesbred and Masham or Suffolk and Blue-Faced Leicester, if you do not appreciate the finer points in the procedure for sheep dipping, and if you are not fully aware of all the possible problems at lambing time, then you are unlikely to make much impression upon George.

His brother Arnold is, by way of variation, interested principally in his hives of bees, which are near enough to the moors to ensure a fine yield of heather honey. Bees will fly at least three miles to heather, and Arnold's hives are a good deal nearer to it than that. Arnold judges folk by how much they know and understand bees, so that if you do not appreciate the different qualities of Caucasians and Italians, if you cannot recognize a queen excluder, and if you think a 'super' is a Sloane adjective rather than a honey box, then you are likely to struggle in seeking to establish any kind of rapport with Arnold.

I had called to see the brothers one fine June morning to talk to them about the wills they had both been promising to make for years. Meeting them both in the farmyard, I tackled George first.

'Now George, have you decided how you want to leave things?', I asked him.

'Aye well, it teks a bit o' reckonin' up, like', replied George, 'an' Ah've bin busy up tae now wi' t' lambin', tha knows.'

'Have you had a good lambing this year?', I felt obliged to ask.

'Aye lad, there's a fair few gimmers up on yon pasture that'll be reight for breedin' on, an' t' rest 'll soon be mekin' t' grade Ah reckon. If tha's got thy gumboots in t' car tha'll be wantin' to see 'em, like, before tha sets off back tae Denley. We've dun reight well wi' twins this year, but Ah were disappointed, like, wi' one o' my Texel yows, that one Ah pointed out to thee t' last time tha landed 'ere. She looked big enuff to bust but when it came to it, like, there were nobbut a single. But mind yer, she's t' biggest gimmer lamb Ah ivver did see.'

By this time George was warming to his subject, so I turned to his brother Arnold in the hopes of making some progress.

'What about you, Arnold, have you any thoughts about your will since we talked last time?'

'Well lad', replied Arnold, 'tha kept bees once ovver if Ah remembers reight, so tha should ken that Ah've bin busy wi' t' hives. It were that wet in t' spring o' t' year that t' bees were jus' not gittin t' chance to fly, an' Ah were still feedin' t' beggars wi' sugar reight up to t' end o' last month. T' last two weeks it's bin that warm an thundery, like, that Ah've bin 'ard put to it to keep up wi' all t' swarms.'

Hearing Arnold say that reminded me of some of the splendid swarms I managed to take in my beekeeping days, and of the old adage that 'a swarm of bees in June is worth a silver spoon', so I said to him:

'You must be pleased, Arnold, if you've managed to hive one or two strong swarms.'

'Nay, Mr Francis, its all reight if tha's theer on t' spot, like, but Ah've missed all t' best swarms. Ah wish Ah could jus' tell t' beggars when tae swarm an' wheer tae land. Ah well remember t' day five years back when Ah took a swarm in yon sycamore tree. That were t' best swarm o' bees Ah ivver took. It were bigger than a rugby ball, an' Ah jus' knocked it down onto t' board in front o' t' hive. T' queen went straight in an' t' rest followed after. It were nobbut a five minute job o' work, Mr Francis. Did them bees work! Ah nivver 'ad such 'eather 'oney out o' one hive for t' past forty year.'

By this time Arnold was well and truly into his stride.

For the next half an hour before I made my excuses and left, I felt rather like a Wimbledon spectator, turning first to my left to listen to sheep talk from George, and then to my right for more of Arnold's beekeeping reminiscences.

Even as I made my way to the car they were both trying to hold my attention as they talked in full flow about their favourite subject.

How much more knowledge will I have to acquire about sheep and bees, I wonder, before I can finally persuade George and Arnold to make their wills?

I don't suppose that city solicitors come into contact with septic tanks too often, either directly or through their clients' title deeds. It is otherwise for country solicitors, and this Saturday morning I have seen them at close quarters on both counts.

First of all I had to inspect a property further up the dale to find out whether the septic tank was within the boundaries of the property or not. After comparing its position with the plan, I decided it was just outside. The deeds were 'silent', as we lawyers say, with regard to any rights to go on the adjoining property to use, maintain and repair it. I had to advise my client that we would need a statutory declaration from the seller that the said tank had been used and 'enjoyed' by owners of his property 'since Adam was a lad'.

I came straight home, changed into my oldest clothes and set out to look at our own septic tank. I had noticed several days previously that the pipes leading to the soakaway had come adrift, and were in urgent need of realignment to stop effluent building up and leaking onto the land. John, my neighbour up the road, came with me. It was my good fortune that his practical know-how was available, for although I am not a bad labourer, I really need a foreman to direct my efforts. We dug out, realigned the pipes and made sure that the system was leakproof, before we covered the pipes and returned home for a glass or two of home-brewed ale.

There is, I think, a satisfaction to be obtained from completing even the simplest of manual jobs, which is just as gratifying as the mastery of some intellectual problem. Society will always need 'hewers of wood and drawers of water', but whenever I join their ranks I am always thankful if I have someone like John to supervise my unskilled efforts. Talk about the plumber's mate!

A conventional septic tank has a settling chamber and a second chamber of the kind that receives the liquid excess that rises to the top. In country districts, the clearing out of accumulated sludge used to be done annually by a pump and tank cart called the 'lavender man', which subsequently spread it on the farmer's fields.

Many Dalesfolk seem to go for years without their septic tanks receiving any attention whatsoever. I rather think that the crafty ones, who don't want to pay for their tanks to be emptied by the council, clean the system now and again by flushing a little yeast or a seaweed product to accelerate oxidisation and bacterial breakdown of the waste material. For some reason, Dales people will not usually admit to this, preferring to attribute the lack of maintenance to the excellent position of their tanks. As a farmer once put it to me:

'Yer see, Mr Francis, if tha's gitten t' lie o' land reight, t' tank'll not tek any fault.'

At all events, I hope that I shall be able to use and 'enjoy' my septic tank for many years, because replacing one is an expensive business.

I groaned inwardly when my secretary Clare told me as soon as I arrived at the office this morning that 'ockard old bugger' Jack Higgins was waiting to see me.

He had certainly not been happy with the result of his accident claim earlier in the year, but it is surprising how even the most dissatisfied people keep turning up again and again.

His mood was clear from the moment he walked into my office.

'Ah 'ope tha'll do a bloody sight better wi' this job than t' last time Ah were 'ere', he began.

'What can I do for you this morning, Mr Higgins?', I asked in my coldest professional manner, doing my best to ignore this rather unpromising start to our meeting.

'Ah've bin dun good an' proper ovver a kitchen table Ah bought sum weeks back. Ah paid nigh on three 'undred pound to 'ave t' table med for us, like, three 'undred pound Ah tell thee...'

'What's wrong with the table?', I asked quickly.

'Well, in t' fust place, t' shop manager Mr Johnson – 'e's a reight wet weekend that un – tell'd us Ah could expect t' table to be delivered i' six week – but it were seven week short of a day afore it landed.'

I was already feeling strong sympathy for Mr Johnson as Jack's voice started to get louder.

'Ah'm surely entitled to knock summat off t' price for t' late delivery.'

Now I have always tried throughout my practising career to answer questions in the language of the layman rather than the lawyer, but on this occasion I decided to give Jack a technical reply.

'Was it expressly agreed in the contract that time was of the essence?'

Jack's face reddened with anger and his voice became even louder.

'There tha goes prattlin' on like a bloody lawyer agin', he exploded, 'as Ah tell'd thee afore, Johnson said it would be six weeks an' that were it – it weren't i' writin' or owt.'

'Then in my opinion, Mr Higgins, you are not entitled to any reduction in price simply because the table was delivered six days later than you expected.'

Jack looked darkly at me. Then with a triumphant leer he tried another tack.

'Well, forget about t' late delivery for t' present. Ah've got yon buggers anyroad.'

'How's that?', I asked.

'Well, t' table Ah ordered were six foot by three, but when Ah checked t' measurement, like, it were a tenth of an inch short, Tha can cum an' measure up thisen, Mr Francis, an' tha'll find Ah'm reight. Ah've got t' buggers theer, an' they're not gittin' away wi' it.'

I gave Jack the lawyer's answer again.

'It sounds to me like a clear case of *de minimis*.'

'What the bloody 'ell is that?', asked Jack, by this time looking as if he could burst a blood vessel at any moment.

'It means, Mr Higgins, that the law does not concern itself with trivialities.'

'Trivialities! Trivialities!', thundered Jack in a voice which must have been heard all over the office. 'Well Ah can see Ah'm wastin' me time 'ere agin', he added, as he stood up and banged a large horny fist down on my desk.

Jack stormed out of my office. I could still hear him uttering expletives as he made his way down the stairs.

I was still shaking my head when Clare came in to tell me about my next appointment.

'They're dead right about Jack Higgins up the dale', I said. 'He is an "ockard old bugger".'

'You can't please everyone all the time', said Clare philosophically.

Secretaries, I often think, are very good at helping solicitors to see clients in their proper perspective, for in truth the 'ockard' ones, like Jack Higgins, are the exception. If that were not the case I would have tried to find another way of earning a living many years ago.

It is the last Saturday morning of the month, and I have spent it mowing my lawns and gathering strawberries.

I smile to myself as I contemplate the lawns, for they are full of clover, yarrow, plantain and daisies. I reflect on how different they are to the prize front lawn which belonged to the father of one of my school friends whom I used to visit in the holidays. There was never a weed on that famous lawn, and its green sward was always smooth and perfect as a billiards table. We boys were not allowed to walk on it or even touch it. Cricket there was out of the question, and had to be played instead on some rough ground beyond the garden.

My lawns are about as far removed from that one as it is possible to imagine. They are played on and walked on. They are the surface for football, roundball, putting and sunbathing, and for exercising the dogs. I never spend a penny on fertiliser or weedkiller, and I shall certainly never be the owner of the manicured lawns which characterise suburban gardens.

What does it matter if there are daisies and clover in a lawn? Clover attracts bees to the garden, and the daisy is such a pretty little flower, reminding me of the chains we made with them as small children, the last link in the chain always being the most difficult to complete.

The daisy, or more literally the 'day's eye', comes in a number of varieties. The one which grows abundantly in my lawns has a number of cousins elsewhere in the garden, in particular those two splendid space-filling herbal daisies, camomile and feverfew. I think it was my Auntie Jane, teacher of almost everything I know about wild flowers, who used to quote to me the teasing rhyme:

> 'The difference I never knew
> Twixt camomile and feverfew.
> I always answer with a smile
> Tis feverfew or camomile.'

Having cut the lawn and trimmed the edges ('Owd Jacob' always insisted that this job hadn't been properly finished unless the edges were done), I feel justified in spending a little time before lunch gathering strawberries.

I am convinced every year that growing strawberies on a small scale is not worth the effort. By the time you have prepared the bed, weeded it, mucked it, laid the straw down, banged in posts, run wires around and draped the protective bird netting over them – in my case, managing to tear off any buttons on my clothing in the process – it would have been far easier to buy some strawberries from the nearest shop, particularly when you discover later that blackbirds have still managed to find a way under the netting, and what they have left the slugs have finished off.

This year I took particular care with the netting and the birds did not get in. I may have defeated the birds for once, but I had not reckoned on a squirrel biting clean through the netting and helping himself. This squirrel was observed by my wife one morning as we were getting dressed.

'Look darling', Rosemary called to me, 'there's a squirrel sitting in the middle of the strawberry bed with a large ripe strawberry between its paws. Isn't he sweet?'

As I stood at the window witnessing the defeat of all my efforts, I must confess that other adjectives came to mind. There are, however, times when an Englishman, particularly if he is a gardener, must try to keep a stiff upper lip. The squirrel and the slugs may have not left many strawberries for me to gather this Saturday morning, but there are after all the raspberries to look forward to next month.

Chapter Seven

'The English winter – ending in July
To recommence in August.'

                                        Lord Byron

My quotation for the month is arguably a slight exaggeration, but it is
the unpredictability of our seasons and weather which is so fascinating
and which provides us all with a reliable topic of conversation. At all
events, it is melancholy to reflect that the longest day of the year has
come and gone all too quickly, and our midsummer night's dream
has passed for another year.

There is always, I think, one special and magical day every year
when the garden is at its very best, equalled only by the wild garden
which lies in the countryside beyond. That day usually falls sometime
in the month of July. This year, it being a 'forward' season, that day
has fallen right at the very start of the month.

The roses are now in full bloom, the borders, bedding-out plants
– particularly my favourites, nemesia and night-scented stock – are
a delight of colour and fragrance, and in the background there is a
gentle humming of bees and the persistent call of wood pigeons in the
woods below. There are flowers, too, in abundance along the verges
on our road, whilst up the dale the colourful meadow flowers which
will disappear with the forthcoming haymaking provide a striking
example of pre-glacial flora. In nearby woods, where we used to
take the children for picnics, there is the unmistakable fragrance of
lily of the valley, whilst down by the river the scent of wild garlic
is all-pervading.

As I contemplate the flowers, I am forever conscious of their
delightful names: heartsease and meadowsweet, love-in-a-mist and
jack-by-the-hedge, creeping jenny and ragged robin, lords and ladies,
lady's bedstraw and evening campion. It is, I think, a happy fact that
these lovely names were not given to flowers by eminent botanists,
but by ordinary country folk centuries ago. In his famous poem about

Lob, the poet Edward Thomas imagined such a countryman:

'Calling the wild cherry tree the merry tree
The rose campion Bridget-in-her-bravery
And in a tender mood he, as I guess
Christened one flower Love-in-idleness
And while he walked from Exeter to Leeds
One April called all cuckoo flowers Milkmaids
From him old herbal Gerard learned, as a boy
To name wild clematis the Traveller's joy . . . '

Days like this, when the garden is perfect and the countryside so
pastoral, should be savoured, for they will all too soon be gone and
the evenings will start to draw in. There is particular pleasure for me
at this time of year in taking a walk just as darkness starts to fall. The
scent of lavender and honeysuckle, always strongest at night, follows
me as I walk down the lane beyond the garden gate. The hedgerows
and ditches rustle with the hidden wildlife, the creatures who dare
to venture out only in the dark. Night is the hunting and courting
time of larger animals and, as the moon and stars paint their heavenly
poetry, owls are hooting and bats are flying.

To contemplate the night sky is always to feel an acute sense of
proportion of one's own importance in the universe, but also to reflect
upon the miracle of life itself. At such times, I am always reminded
of the words of that fine country writer, George Borrow, who loved
the romany life:

'There's night and day, brother, both sweet things: sun, moon and
stars, brother, all sweet things; there's likewise a wind on the heath.
Life is very sweet, brother . . . '

'Lucky Jim' was back in the office this month, with another tale of
woe.

'Ah reckoned Ah'd gitten mysen a reet bargain, Mr Francis', he
began. 'T' missus an' me 'ave allus wanted a pair o' statues, like, to
set off t' garden – tha knows, t' soart tha sees in t' Italian gardens at
Scarborough – and theer they were in a shop Ah were just passin' at
Ghylldale t' other day, They nobbut cost me a tenner for t' pair, an'
Ah were on me way, like, afore t' shopkeeper could change 'is mind.
T' missus were 'ighly delighted an' all. But them statues 'adn't bin in

t' garden for two days when t' police landed an' asked if they could 'ave a word wi' me i' private, like. *Unfortunately, Mr Francis, it turns out that them statues 'ad bin stolen from a garden in bloody Ilkley. T' owners want 'em back an' t' police 'ave tekken 'em away. Ah reckon Ah've paid good money for them statues, Mr Francis, so what Ah wants to know is . . . what dus t' law 'ave to say on t' subject, like?'*

I answered Jim with just five words:

'Nemo dat quod non habet.'

'Yer what?', he retorted.

I attempted to explain the Latin maxim which governs this area of law.

' "Nobody can give what he doesn't own" ', I said. 'The law says that you cannot pass a legal title in goods to someone else if you haven't got a legal title to them in the first place. The shopkeeper apparently bought the statues from a thief or a receiver, so he was in no position to sell them on to you. My advice is to agree to the police returning them to their original owners, and then try to get your money back from the shopkeeper.'

'Nay, Mr Francis, its not t' tenner Ah'm bothered about, it's t' statues Ah wants – an' so dus t' missus an' all', replied Jim.

'I'm sorry, Mr Bottomley, but you won't be able to get them back from the police this side of the court case, and as I've said I don't believe you will ever be entitled to their return. Mind you, things could have been different if you'd bought the statues in *market overt.*'

'What the 'angment's that?', asked Jim.

'Its literal meaning is an "open market", Mr Bottomley, but it doesn't apply in your case because you bought the statues from a shop. I'm sorry, but the law in your case seems quite clear and it's not on your side.'

As Jim left the office I was left smiling to myself, not just about Jim's further disaster, but also about an old story which Yorkshire solicitors are wont to tell and which came to mind as the facts of Jim's case unfolded.

The story goes that, at the old Halifax quarter sessions in bygone days, there were two rather pompous barristers standing in the robing room, where they were holding an erudite discussion on the subject of Einstein's Theory of Relativity. Also in the same room and reclining in a comfortable armchair was a very stolid-looking Halifax solicitor, reading his *Yorkshire Post* and smoking his pipe. After a little while, one of the barristers turned to him and said, somewhat patronisingly:

'Tell me, my friend and I would be most interested to know, what is your opinion of Einstein's Theory of Relativity?'

The Halifax solicitor looked up, put his paper to one side and slowly removed his pipe from his mouth before replying:

'I reckon nowt to it, nor his ruddy statues neither!'

The pitfalls of home-made wills are many. They are not always obvious to non-lawyers, and sometimes the wishes of the person making such a will can be thwarted, with results which are the very opposite of the those intended. I have had two such cases in the office this month.

Elderly widow Daisy Buxton made her own will. In it she left 'all my money invested in the Halifax Building Society to my godson James', and 'all my money invested in the Abbey National Building Society to my goddaughter Fiona'. The residue of the estate she left to her only son Peter.

At the time the will was made there had been £5,000 in each building society account, but some time later she had decided to close her Abbey National account and had used the money to buy some Treasury stock. Daisy never bothered to change her will, believing that the money previously invested with the building society would still go to Fiona. As it was, I had to advise Fiona, following Daisy's death, that the money invested in Treasury stock formed part of the residue of the estate and legally belonged to Peter.

Now all would have still been well if Peter had done the decent thing and honoured his mother's intentions – for many things are possible by agreement – but he had heartily disliked Fiona from the time they were children, and she had once bowled him out first ball for a duck in a family cricket match on Scarborough beach.

'What's mine is mine', he said simply, and that was that.

'I'm sorry Fiona, but there's nothing I can do about it. If only your godmother had instructed a solicitor to make her will', I said, after telling her of Peter's attitude.

The second disastrous home-made will I came across this month arose when a man called Norman Stephenson married a woman called Shirley, following the dissolution of his first marriage. It was 'second time around' for her as well, and they both had grown-up children from their previous marriages.

They were both living in London, and decided to move up North to make a fresh start. They employed a London solicitor to act on their behalf in buying a house in Denley. The house was bought in their joint names, and the conveyance contained a declaration that they held the property as 'joint tenants'.

Their London solicitor, however, had not discussed with them what their respective positions would be in the event of a death. Norman and Shirley both wanted their share of the house to go to their own children, and had each completed will forms to this effect without taking any legal advice.

Shortly after the couple moved to Denley, Norman died suddenly of a heart attack. His son and daughter came in to see me to enquire about their legal position. I had the unhappy task of telling them that, in law, their father's share in the house passed to his wife Shirley by virtue simply of her having survived him. The home-made will was ineffective to carry out Norman's wishes. Shirley had never cared much for Norman's own family, and she quickly made it clear that she intended to apply the strict letter of the law. The house was hers and hers alone.

An old farming friend, Bert Riding, called in to see me last Sunday just as Rosemary had made a pot of tea.

'Aye, lad, Ah'll just 'ave a toothful', said Bert, when I offered him a cup.

I often remember people not so much for their legal problems, but by their favourite words and expressions. The other memorable word Bert once used, when describing the fancy food he had been offered at some rather posh function, was 'muckment', a description with which we Yorkshiremen, who like simple home cooking without any frills, will heartily agree.

Bert's vicar before last was best remembered not for the spiritual blessings he bestowed upon his flock, but for his frequent and often inappropriate use of his favourite expression, 'by golly'.

There was one occasion, never forgotten in the village, when he visited a very well-loved elderly widow in the parish.

'Would you like another piece of my walnut cake, vicar?', she politely asked him.

'No, by golly, I've had some', he replied.

I shall forever remember Edith Hetton for using what she obviously thought were impressive and weighty words, but which she tended to get slightly wrong.

'Of all the audocity', she once said of a cheeky neighbour; and another time, remarking on recent windy weather, she observed, 'the wind's debating'.

I deplore the trend which seems to be in vogue of following the American pattern of using christian names at all times and on all occasions, no matter how short the acquaintance. I am forever coming into my office to find messages on my desk, asking me to phone 'Julie' at this building society or 'Debbie' from that bank.

It is even worse when clients are at the receiving end of such forward attitudes. I had a meeting recently with an old friend, George Farnley, to discuss various matters relating to his family farm. George invited a young 'whizz kid' accountant whom his bank manager had recommended. Now I have no doubt that the young accountant is a very able professional, but when he began a sentence at an early stage in the meeting with 'Now, tell me George . . . ', I felt embarrassed. Whilst it would have been natural for me to have called George by his christian name, since I had known him from being a boy, coming as it did from a young accountant meeting him for the first time, it seemed both ill-mannered and patronising. George looked decidedly uncomfortable.

Over the years I have been called many different names from time to time, but there are two which I particularly dislike. The first is 'young man', which would be flattering if it were not clearly sarcastic; and the second is 'squire', a term beloved by secondhand car salesmen.

It has always struck me as both strange and amusing that when you describe the kind of car you wish to buy, such a salesman will invariably reply:

'They're like gold, squire, they're like gold.'

However, his reaction to the car you wish to sell will always be:

'We've got a yard full of those, squire. We can't give 'em away, squire, we can't give 'em away.'

I still know just one or two people who still use the slang of the Second World War, and who always call me 'old boy'. Johnny Mason had been an RAF pilot, and when he talked to me about the war it was always of friends who had 'gone for a Burton', or about old so-and-so having 'bought it over the drink'. Rather curiously for an RAF type, he tended to use naval expressions at the table.

'I say, old boy, would you mind giving the cruets a fair wind in my direction', he once said to me over lunch at the Denley Heifer.

Johnny had been a keen fisherman all his life but, as happens to ageing anglers, he found it increasingly difficult to tie his trout flies properly, and really needed a younger companion to help him.

'We really must have a day's fishing together sometime, old boy', he said to me on his last visit to the office.

A few days later came news of his death, We shall not see his like again. I am not sure whether our young people fully appreciate that they owe the freedom they enjoy to Johnny and fellow pilots who saved England during the Battle of Britain, when we stood absolutely alone. At any rate, when I next go down to the river, I shall delay casting for a few minutes and just contemplate as I quietly remember Johnny. I shall miss you . . . old boy.

Humour in letters which pass between solicitors is rare, and so is all the more welcome when it is to be found.

Earlier this month, I was acting on behalf of a great friend of mine, Dick Wrenbeck, in the sale of his house on the outskirts of Denley. The purchaser's solicitor asked me to confirm that Dick's property had mains drains.

As luck would have it, my secretary Clare – who has been extremely adept over the years at interpreting my sometimes wayward dictation and handwriting – was away on holiday. The 'temp', Mandy, whom I had engaged in her absence, misheard my dictation, which was meant to read:

'We confirm that the property has mains drainage.'

She typed instead:

'We confirm that the property has monies drainage.'

*Un*fortunately, as 'Lucky Jim' would have said, I did not notice the mistake before the letter went out.

Opening the post at the office every morning is a time-consuming and sometimes a rather boring and depressing affair, but the morning I received a reply to this letter was considerably brightened. I could not help laughing out loud when I read:

'Please reconsider your reply to our question. Our client fully appreciates that maintaining property is an expensive business these days, but he really cannot afford to throw money down the drain.'

I have managed to keep the blackbirds out of the strawberry bed for the most part, but I have not been so successful with my four rows of raspberries, where they have certainly enjoyed more than their fair share. One of the pleasures of growing soft fruit on a small scale and for pleasure is that you can choose varieties which are not produced commercially but which have the best flavour, and I keep experimenting to this end.

For a gardener like myself who is also a bit of an entomologist, it is interesting and comforting, however, to observe that whatever varieties I select, yellow underwing moths still fly up from strawberry beds, and the charming little magpie moth is often disturbed when I am among the raspberry canes or gooseberry bushes.

I also grow the loganberry, that splendid cross between raspberry and blackberry, and train it on runners against a sunny wall. It is a strange fact that this juicy, dark red fruit is hardly ever touched by the birds; which is a bonus, for, perhaps of all the soft fruits, loganberries make the best jam, a treat on toast to contemplate on some cold afternoon next winter when we have tea around a log fire.

Talking of soft fruit, there is one annual ritual which is still to be undertaken before the end of the month – the expedition we always make at this time of year to gather wild bilberries high on the moors.

Surely there can be no more tedious job in this world than trying to gather a quantity of this particular fruit, for the berries are generally small, very well-concealed and come away from the bushes with the greatest difficulty imaginable. You tend in your frustration to end up squashing many of them, which invariably results in badly-stained fingers, and if you are tempted, as I usually am, to eat one or two berries raw, your mouth will look as if it has been treated with gentian violet.

Quite near home there are several large colonies of the green hairstreak butterfly, its dull grey appearance disguising the brilliant green undersides of its wings. The sole reason the species is found on the moors is because its food plant is the wild bilberry. I am inclined to think that the plant should be left to the butterflies.

In the meantime I dream of the year when, on our annual bilberry expedition, I have at my command a score of sharp-eyed children who will, in no time at all, fill their containers to the brim with exceptionally large, juicy berries which are so ripe that they have virtually dropped off the bushes. The only part I play in the dream is to direct operations and to feast on the ensuing freshly-made bilberry pie. Surely it can only be the prospect of that mouthwatering pie which compels us every year to gather bilberries high up on the nearby moors.

Although, as I have written earlier, matrimonial difficulties seem to be particularly prevalent just after Christmas, it is a sad fact of modern family life that divorce is becoming more and more common, and in every month of the year.

I have noticed too, that, there have been some profound changes to the manner in which divorce cases are conducted, partly no doubt because of the dramatic increase in women solicitors over the past few years.

I have the greatest possible respect and admiration for lady solicitors, including the three at Boothroyd and Lytton, who are an invaluable part of our firm. Indeed one has been a trusted colleague of mine for nearly thirty years.

There are a few, however, who bring to the practice of the law, some views and attitudes very different from those of the traditional family solicitor, and which are clearly attributable, at least in part, to the changing role of women in society generally.

Earlier this month I was consulted by Jimmy Dobson, whose wife Sandra had walked out on him to live with another man, leaving behind their three year old son and a baby daughter who was barely six months old.

Jimmy came into my office in a state of considerable distress and asked if, as a first step, I would contact his wife's solicitor to see whether there was any chance of a reconciliation. This I was only too glad to do, for it has always seemed to me to be the prime duty of a solicitor to seek reconciliation rather than litigation, particularly in divorce cases.

I telephoned Sandra's solicitor who, as it transpired, was a newly-qualified woman lawyer. After telling her of Jimmy's distress at the situation and of his desire for a reconciliation, I said to her in my rather old-fashioned way:

'Don't you think that in the interests of these two very young children that their mother should consider returning home to look after them?'

Her reply was curt and challenging.

'Why do you assume that my client should be at home? Why can't your client look after them?'

No amount of explanation from me about Jimmy's obvious difficulties at work, or of the strain placed upon his elderly parents in helping him to cope with two very small children, was going to alter her views.

It seems to me, as I reflect upon these changing attitudes, that traditional family life is likely to come under increasing threat, not least because the inestimable value of women as wives and mothers continues to be so shamefully downgraded. I have often thought that if men put half as much time and effort into their family life as into their careers, and if women concentrated as much on homemaking as on 'fulfilling themselves', then divorce would not be nearly so common. One thing is absolutely certain: it is the children who invariably suffer most when a marriage breaks down.

Divorce is very much easier to obtain nowadays. My impression gained from handling many matrimonial cases over the years is that too many young couples rush off to their lawyers for a quick divorce when the first serious difficulty in their marriage arises, rather than working together to overcome the problem and emerge with their relationship strengthened.

On the other hand, I would not care to see the law return to the days when society insisted on the maintenance of a marriage which had clearly broken down. I am in any case doubtful whether the success rate of marriage in days gone by was any higher. I well remember my grandmother once telling me that many of her friends had unhappy or unsatisfactory marriages, and would undoubtedly have sued for divorce had they not been economically dependent upon their husbands. Such constraints, of course, no longer apply or not at any rate to anything like the same extent.

It is often said that the two main causes of divorce are money and sex – not necessarily in that order – but I don't know whether this is altogether true. To have too little money can of course present severe difficulties, yet some of the happiest married couples I have known have been the poorest, and it is a fact that marriage breakdown occurs frequently in wealthy couples and amongst the aristocracy.

As for sex, my own view, for what it is worth, is that there is altogether too much fuss made about the subject, that the physical side of a marriage is likely to be a reflection of its spiritual quality, and that if you are honest, loving and sensitive, or if you can combine

95

any two of those qualities with a sense of humour, you will have a perfectly good sex life. From my own observation of divorce cases, I would say that adultery alone is rarely the sole cause of a marriage breakdown, but rather the symptom of an unhappy relationship.

I have just put away in our strongroom a divorce file which has been in my cabinet for twelve years. During this time the parties concerned have repeatedly fought over issues of custody, access, property, maintenance and financial matters generally, with every court order made from time to time being the subject of an appeal. It has all cost them both dearly in terms of time and money.

Life is too short, I reflected, as I removed the file – at the same time being conscious of the fact that, on present trends at any rate, the matrimonial lawyer is never likely to go short of work!

I shall remember for a long time to come the occasion this month when Bertie 'know-all' Smith finally got his come-uppance.

Bertie had put me to shame earlier in the year, when I had visited his farm to discuss a tax saving scheme upon which he had considerably improved; just as he had, over the years, run rings around doctors, accountants, vets and various representatives of officialdom.

I was journeying up the dale to see one of Bertie's neighbours. I had just turned on to the minor road which runs past Bertie's farm, when I was brought to an abrupt halt by a herd of cows being driven along the road towards an entrance to a field about fifty yards away.

The old farmer driving the herd was tapping the cows at the back with a stick, and he was being helped in keeping the procession orderly by two sheepdogs, one at each side of the road.

At first I did not recognise the farmer, for he had his back towards me, but, as soon as he heard my car braking, he turned around.

Bertie and I recognised each other straight away. He gave me a cheery wave and slapped one of his cows on the backside. As he did so, he looked at me with a self-satisfied expression which clearly said:

'Watch on, lad, if tha wants to see sum beasts driven t' reight way.'

Now I learnt very early in life, when I started to play cricket, that you should never take your eye off the ball. Bertie was about to appreciate just how true this was.

As he turned back to face his cows, he discovered that the hand he had rested on the cow's rump was now generously covered with that noxious substance that is prone to emerge from a cow's backside at

regular intervals. Bertie's expression changed from self-satisfaction to disgust as he felt the smelly liquid trickle down his arm, and quickly pulled it away.

A solicitor should not laugh at any client's discomfort, but I could not help myself from literally shaking with laughter as I followed Bertie and his cows along the road.

He finally got his herd into the field, shut the gate, and was doing his best to wipe his arm clean with a bunch of grass he had picked up by the roadside, as I honked my horn and proceeded on my journey.

It was now my turn to give a cheery wave.

Confined as I am to an office desk for much of my working days, I often think of the words of Richard Jefferies' *Gamekeeper at Home:*

'It's indoors, sir, as kills half the people, being indoors three parts of the day, and next to that taking too much drinks and vittals. Eating's as bad as drinking; and there ain't nothing like fresh air and the smell of the woods.'

After a week in the office, the weekend is a time to be savoured. On the last Saturday of the month, I decided to forsake the garden and all the jobs around the house which needed attention to go off on my own for a ramble around the countryside, a pleasure which is all too rare these days.

I always find it a good idea to have some sort of objective in view on such a walk. It may be a wild flower to identify, a bird to look for or a village church to visit, but I decided for this walk to search for the white letter hairstreak butterfly, traditionally associated with elm trees and which has been gradually distributed northwards since the advent of Dutch elm disease ravaged the south of England.

We are fortunate in the Dales in possessing many fine deciduous trees and tracts of ancient woodland. In some parts of the country where there is still such woodland left, it provides a home for the stag beetle, the nightingale and the dormouse, but when I reach the local wood fringed with large old elm trees, my eyes will principally be alerted to the hope of seeing the small, dark-coloured butterfly which is the white letter hairstreak.

There is a walk through a small village before I reach the wood, and as I entered the village, some boys were playing football in a field next to the playground. My mind waxed indignant. What sacrilege for Yorkshire boys to be playing football during the cricket season! This thought, however, did not stop me from joining in the game for a few minutes and pretending, to myself at any rate, that I was some latter-day Stanley Matthews or Tom Finney.

At the far end of the village, by the bridge over the river, I came across a sight to gladden my heart. Two boys were trout fishing, and from the colourful floats bobbing around downstream, I guessed they were both bottom fishing with worms.

'Any luck?', I whispered as I approached them.

'Not yet, mister, we've only just started', replied one of them.

I stood for a few minutes watching them, remembering as I did so my own fishing expeditions at their age, and of the first trout I caught, unforgettable, all silvery with brilliant red spots and borne home in triumph.

About a mile beyond the river bridge is the village cricket field, and as the players took to the field in the golden afternoon sunshine, resplendent in their white shirts and flannel trousers, I paused for a moment to capture in my mind the scene unfolding before me and to realise again that cricket is an extraordinarily English game.

When I reached my woodland destination at last, I could not help noticing that the field in front of it was a classic example of bad husbandry. There were hundreds of thistles, the flowers of which were being settled upon by large numbers of newly-emerged small tortoiseshell butterflies; and literally thousands of ragwort, the foliage of which was covered by a crawling mass of the caterpillars of the cinnabar moth. This caterpillar seems totally immune to the ragwort, which is poisonous to sheep and cattle, although curiously not in the spring if it is eaten before it has the chance to grow.

I wondered whether farmers are cutting down on the use of pesticides and chemicals, for all manner of wild flowers seem to be commoner this year, particularly the delightful red poppy, the presence of which, like ragwort, is a sure sign of a hungry soil. It would be a duller countryside, I think, which could not find field or two for ragwort and poppy.

I walked carefully through the woodland rich in trees, flowers, birds and various species of butterfly. It is the sort of place where you can imagine lady's slipper orchids, goldcrests, scotch argus butterflies and any number of other rarities being present – but of the white letter hairstreak there was no sign.

On a stile at the end of the wood I paused for a while, lit my pipe, contemplated the pastoral scene and said aloud those well-known lines of W H Davies:

'What is this life if full of care
We have no time to stand and stare?'

I decided to make my way home by a different route. About half a mile from my garden gate, my eye was suddenly caught by some movement high up in a large old elm tree at the the side of the road. On close inspection I found myself, unbelievably, looking at a pair of white letter hairstreaks flying joyously in the late afternoon sunshine. Here, then, was my elusive quarry living right on my own doorstep. What a triumphant end to my summer ramble, and how exciting and pleasing to find that we have such delightful neighbours. But then it so often happens in life, doesn't it, that the nicest things happen when you are least expecting them.

Chapter Eight

'*August for the people and their favourite islands.*'
W H Auden

I often think that the French, who traditionally down tools and go off on holiday for the whole of this month, are very wise. They really put Auden's line into practice, yet here am I at the beginning of the month still slaving away in my stuffy office, whilst in my garden I am confronted by a plague of greenfly and other aphids which have multiplied alarmingly following a recent hot spell. It is as well, then, that ladybirds, those delightful little aphid-eating beetles, seem to be especially abundant this year.

I wonder whether country children still coax a ladybird to crawl onto their outstretched hands, and say aloud, as we used to do:

'Ladybird, ladybird, fly away home.
Your house is on fire, your children all gone.'

We children also regarded it as a special find if we came across black ladybirds, either the yellow-spotted or the red-spotted variety. Such an event was as rare and exciting as finding a four-leafed clover.

Looking at all the ladybirds in the garden set me thinking about beetles generally, and to conclude how very little I, and probably most people, know about them. I am ashamed to admit that I can only recognise a handful of the 3,500 different species reckoned to be found in this country.

I know the blue-black oil beetle which I turn up from time to time with my garden fork; the antlered stag beetle, the flea beetle and the burying beetle are familiar to me; and so are the water beetles, the whirligigs which whizz round like dodgem cars in a fairground, and which I remember from boyhood days when we looked for yellow-underbellied newts in ponds. I know, as I

101

should do in our farming country, the dor beetle that lays its eggs in cowpats. I have heard the death watch beetle, which is the cause of many an appeal for church restoration funds; and I also know that wretched little fellow, the common furniture beetle, which the specialist woodworm companies find so unerringly in their surveys and which they prefer to call by its Latin name of *Anobium punctatum* in their impressive-sounding reports.

I have to confess that, even as a countryman interested in all forms of natural history, my own knowledge of beetles does not go much beyond those I have mentioned, but there is a certain client of mine, one Ferdinand Ribston, who knows a great deal more.

Whenever I see 'Ferdy', as he is known by his friends, he is inevitably dressed in the same rather loud checked suit, always with a bow tie and wearing half-moon spectacles, looking for all the world like an absent-minded university professor. His lifetime hobby has been the study of beetles, or coleoptera as he prefers to call them, and he talks to me passionately about them whenever he has the chance.

As a bachelor, Ferdy has had plenty of time to pursue his hobby, which involves - amongst other things - digging around tree stumps at the dead of night, an activity which, I would have thought, was an unlikely sounding excuse for trespass should he ever be challenged.

I suppose that all natural historians tend to regard their own branch of study as intellectually superior, and Ferdy is no exception. He knows that I am interested in lepidoptera (butterflies) and to a lesser extent in neuroptera (dragonflies). When we chat, as we sometimes do, about the respective merits of our particular interests, his invariable parting shot is to quote Oliver Wendell Holmes from *The poet at the breakfast table:*
    'Lepidoptera and Neuroptera for little folks
    but Coleoptera for men, sir!'

I have been having problems again this month with clients' wills, or rather with notes which they have made which are intended to be read in conjunction with them.

Old Enid Armitage had made a will with me in which she left her cottage and all its contents to her sister Beryl, with the rest of her estate to be shared equally between certain charities. This should have been simple enough, but Beryl – who along with myself was Enid's executor – found among her sister's papers a lengthy list of some house contents, with directions that upon her death they should go to certain named relatives.

Beryl came into my office, showed me her sister's list and asked for my advice. I started reading. According to Enid's directions, there was a silver teapot to go to her niece Jayne, a carriage clock to nephew Paul, a set of dining room chairs to her godson James and a crown Derby collection to her cousin Janet. I glanced quickly through the rest of the list, which contained a score or so of similar requests, and I turned to Beryl.

'These notes are of no legal validity whatsoever', I said to her. 'The entire contents of Enid's cottage are yours under the terms of her will.'

'Yes, Mr Francis', she replied rather hesitantly, 'but isn't there a moral obligation on me to honour my sister's wishes?'

'Well, that really is a matter entirely for you, Miss Armitage, but I should warn you that you may well find that there's less gratitude than you might expect.'

Sure enough, only two days later Beryl was back in the office – but this time she was in tears. It was a few minutes and a cup of coffee later before she had recovered her composure sufficiently to speak.

'I felt I ought to honour my sister's wishes, Mr Francis, but now I'm not so sure. Jayne doesn't want the silver teapot because she says she has quite enough silver to clean already; Paul was disappointed because he thought he was getting my sister's grandfather clock; James says he doesn't want any more chairs; and Janet seemed to blame me because she wasn't getting a diamond ring she was expecting in addition to the crown Derby.'

She paused for a moment.

'I'm really very sorry', I replied, 'but I did warn you this might happen. Perhaps it would be simpler for you to stick to the terms of your sister's will and ignore the notes.'

'I think that's just what I shall do now Mr Francis, but it seems such a shame.'

Even worse for an executor is where there is not a written note, as in Enid's case, but a supposed verbal request by the deceased that somebody is to benefit under his or her will.

Fred Fothergill appointed myself and his only surviving relative, cousin Alfred, to be his executor. After his death we met at his home to sort out Fred's possessions. As we were right in the middle of this job, there was a knock at the door and

Fred's neighbour, Charlie Bradshaw, popped his head round the corner.

'Na then, Ah've jus bethought mysen', Charlie said, 'an' Ah reckons tha'd best be knowin'. Aboot a fortneet afore 'e died, Fred tell'd me straight that if owt shoud 'appen to 'im, like, then 'e wanted me to look after 'is gardenin' tools for 'im. Ah were jus' sayin' to t' missus that two men 'ad landed at Fred's place to tek t' job in hand, an' t' pair on us reckoned they ought to be put in t' picture, like, ovver t' matter o' t' gardenin' tools.'

At that point Charlie stopped talking and looked at us as if expecting an instant response.

Despite my own reservations, cousin Alfred insisted that we give Charlie all Fred's old spades, forks and trowels. But when Charlie, no doubt encouraged by this success, approached us both again only half an hour later to say that Fred had asked him to 'look after' his coin collection and 'set o' gold sovereigns an' all', I could not resist giving Alfred an 'I told you so' look. This time Alfred would have none of it, and rapidly sent Charlie packing.

The truth is that notes and verbal requests simply won't do. That is why I always encourage people to make proper wills, not only in my interests but in their interests and that of their families as well.

This is a difficult month in which to conduct a legal practice. Partners and staff are often on holiday, their work still has to be done and our half-strength office is at full stretch.

Some clients are on holiday too, and it never ceases to amaze me how many of them choose to be out of the country at a critical point in their cases. It is for instance no easy task, and one which I have just had to perform, to contact a client who is cruising among certain undisclosed Greek islands in order to take instructions upon a suggested completion date for his house sale.

Holidays anywhere – but particularly abroad – can prove a mixed blessing, but any disasters can of course produce work for solicitors.

Over the past few years I have had a steady flow of cases arising from holiday experiences, the worst being one last year which I have only just settled. My clients' hotel on the Costa del somewhere-or-other had turned out to be half-completed and overbooked, which meant that they had to spend the first two days at another hotel, miles from anywhere. It would perhaps have been better if they had stayed there, for when they were eventually taken to the original hotel they found that the grounds resembled a building site, the swimming pool was filled with rubble, there were cockroaches in many of the rooms and there was a shooting range immediately to the side of the hotel – which made it hazardous to say the least for them to allow their small children to play outside unsupervised!

On the very day earlier this week when I finally settled the hotel case and obtained decent compensation, I was consulted by Sidney and Jessie Baker, who had recently decided for a special treat to spend a weekend in Paris to celebrate their ruby wedding anniversary. On their very first evening in Paris, they had been assaulted and robbed of all their money and cheque cards, as well as their passports, whilst they were making their way from their hotel to a restaurant.

The assault was reported to the police, but their attackers had not been found. Sidney and Jessie's lifetime treat had turned into a nightmare, and they had to obtain the help of the British Embassy to get new passports and ask relatives back home to send them money to enable them to return.

The Common Market – like holidays abroad – is, I think, a mixed blessing. Whilst there is surely everything to be said for political and economic co-operation with our neighbouring countries, I am strongly opposed to surrendering our sovereignty – and in particular to the concept of European law taking precedence over English law. We are an ancient race, an island people and in my opinion we should retain our freedom and our independence.

However, as a lawyer I have to advise on the law as it stands. Upon considering the facts of the Bakers' case and the legal effects of the Treaty of Rome, I was able to advise Sidney and Jessie that they should be able to submit a claim for damages to the Criminal Injuries Compensation Board in Paris.

We shall have to see how I get on with Sidney and Jessie's case. Money cannot of course compensate them for their terrible experience, but it will help a bit. If the French can be encouraged to pay up, then that would be just my idea of how the old *entente cordiale* should work in practice!

Patience is a necessary quality in a solicitor, particularly when trying to bring a client to the subject matter of his case. I have found from experience that you often have to be prepared to jump through a number of widely diverse hoops before he or she will finally get around to giving you instructions.

'Before we get down to business, Mr Francis there's something I must show you', or 'I wonder if you can help me with . . . ', or 'I simply must tell you about . . . ', are just a few of the opening remarks which produce an inward sigh and a realisation that you are likely to be in for a long haul.

Politeness is also a quality that solicitors must cultivate. Over the years, I have found myself involved in many non-legal matters in the course of seeing clients – and for which they most certainly would not expect to be charged, no matter how many units of 'chargeable time' are thrown up on my firm's computer!

I have looked through innumerable family photograph albums; I have endured the showing of many ciné films or videos of foreign holidays (surely there can be nothing quite so tedious in this life than having to watch films of other peoples' holidays, particularly when accompanied by a detailed commentary); I have listened to accounts of illnesses and operations described in excruciating and anatomically shocking detail; I have helped to move furniture, to polish silver and to plant shrubs; I have inspected houses, flats and bungalows; I have walked around farms in all sorts of weather; once I even emptied a chamber pot for a bedridden client!

There was one equally unforgettable occasion when I arrived to see Pat Darrowby, a sheep farmer, right in the middle of dipping time.

'Na then, Mr Francis, tha's landed at just t' reet moment. If tha lends a hand, like, t' sooner t' job's dun an' t' sooner we can get down to business, like.'

'But . . . but . . . Mr Darrowby, I'm not dressed for the job', I protested.

'Nay, Mr Francis' tha's not gittin' away that easy', replied Pat, tossing an old boiler suit in my direction.

Now anyone who has ever taken part in sheep dipping will know that it is not as easy a job as it looks, particularly when it comes to catching and dipping a large ram.

'That un's thine', shouted Pat, pointing to his prize ram.

'Oh no, I'd rather leave the ram to you', I replied hastily, but to no avail.

Pat and his two sons, who had come to help, all had wide grins on their faces as they watched me. Then came the loud guffaws of laughter when, in attempting to control the large ram and steer it into the dip, I lost both my grip and my balance and fell straight into the sheep dip myself.

'Nay, Mr Francis, an' there's me thinkin' tha's 'ad a bit to do wi' stock. Tha'll not tek any fault', Pat added, as he surveyed my appearance. 'But Ah reckons tha'd best cum back another day to discuss t' business, like.'

When I arrived back home, Rosemary looked at me in amazement, sniffed and said:

'You smell of sheep dip, darling.'

It is, I suppose, hardly a smell which a solicitor's wife would expect to notice upon her husband's return from the office.

'I've told you before, darling, nobody – not even you – will ever believe the things a country solicitor has to do to keep his clients happy', I replied with some feeling.

I was telling my old friend and retired Denley GP, Dr Meredith, about the hoops we poor solicitors have to jump through, and he laughed when I recounted my sheep-dipping experience.

'I think I can cap that story, John', he said with a smile. 'When I was a young doctor in wartime, fresh butter was hard to come by, but my wife heard that a certain old farmer's wife, who was also a patient of mine, might be persuaded to spare us a pound or two. So she sent me off to see her. Now she and her husband were known to be staunch Methodists. When I went into the farmhouse, the old lady made me sit down and tell her the reason for my visit. I felt distinctly nervous and ill at ease as I explained my "mission".

"My wife tells me", I said, "that . . . er . . . there . . . er . . . may . . . er . . . er . . . a . . . chance that . . . er . . . you . . . er . . . might have a little . . . er . . . butter to spare."

The old lady said nothing, but after a minute she started playing her harmonium. When she'd played various hymns on it, she suddenly stopped.

"Now doctor", she said in a tone of voice which brooked no argument. "You must now join me in going down on your knees and singing the first three verses of *Count your blessings*."

And that, John, is precisely what I had to do before I came away with my small slab of butter.'

Although I have done many different things for clients, I have not as yet been asked to sing with them. It is just as well, for with my singing voice I could surely not expect to keep them for very long.

It should be one of the perks of being self-employed to be able to take the odd day off to watch a test match at Headingley, to fish one of the local trout rivers or just to enjoy a summer's day in the countryside. But whenever I make such plans, there always seem to be urgent tasks which crop up in the office.

One day this month, however, I actually managed half a day away from work to watch Yorkshire playing a county championship match at Harrogate.

As I stood watching the play on this delightful ground, I found myself thinking of Hutton, Trueman, Yardley, Wardle, Illingworth, Brennan and all the Yorkshire stars of my boyhood, and realised with a shock that the last time I watched a match on this ground was in 1962, when I was part of a proud and excited crowd who saw the Tykes win the county championship.

As I watched I also remembered my own cricketing days, first at my Yorkshire prep school and later at Rossall, the famous public school on the Lancashire coast where one of my heroes, F W Harvey, solicitor, poet, soldier and countryman, also learnt his cricket. He later wrote a famous poem about it called *The Catch*:

'Whizzing fierce it came
Down the summer air
Burning like a flame
On my fingers bare.'

Cricketers who have ever fielded in the slips must surely recognise the feeling expresed in those lines; and those of us who, like Harvey, learnt our cricket on the windswept Fylde coast will surely also recognise his description later in the same poem:

'Rossall on the shore
Where the sea sobs wild
Like a homesick child.'

The very day after my trip to Harrogate, when in the course of a morning's appointments I saw two deserted wives and a young unemployed man who was in tears over a mountain of debt, I thought about Will Harvey again, for he spent most of his practising career representing life's failures and unfortunates. He was famed throughout the Forest of Dean for representing widows facing eviction from their cottages, young men in trouble with the police, or girls who – as he put it – had 'slipped a bit'.

I have often envied Harvey, for he hated being confined to the office, and he was wont to close it on a whim simply to wander the Gloucestershire countryside or to visit his favourite hostelries. He eventually closed his office altogether and retreated to his house in the forest, outside which he erected a sign which said simply:

'F W Harvey. Solicitor and Commissioner for Oaths.'

Harvey always cared more for people than for profit. He neglected his practice - which predictably declined – and he ended his life in some poverty, having to sell off much of his fine library in order to support his family.

He remained, however, to the end of his days a friend to the poor and oppressed, whilst his natural eloquence and mastery of words made him a brilliant advocate in the magistrates courts of West Gloucestershire. Although his personal circumstances sadly deteriorated, he was known as 'Mr Harvey, a learned gentleman' by the ordinary forest people right up to the end of his professional life.

I always feel some affinity with Will Harvey, for not only were we educated at the same school and both became lawyers, but I share with him a love of cricket, the Anglican Church, the English countryside and magistrates court advocacy.

It is a sobering thought that years of legal work and court cases are quickly forgotten, but great writing lives on. If I am ever feeling a bit down, I read Harvey's most famous poem, *Ducks*. There are two particular lines which always make me chuckle:

'Caterpillars and cats are lively and excellent puns.
All God's jokes are good, even the practical ones!'

Robert Tranmere, a good friend from way back, asked me to act for him earlier this month. He had agreed to buy part of a field from his neighbour Sidney Forrest. Robert had told me that Sidney had agreed to sell his field in two lots, one half of it to him and the other half to another neighbour.

After I had written to ask them to send me a draft contract for approval, Sidney's solicitors, Messrs Danby, Loxton and Stott, a city firm which I had never come across previously, wrote me to ask whether I appreciated that 'the two halves were not equal halves'.

I pondered for some little time over this puzzling question, before replying that indeed I had not appreciated it, and in any case the wording of his letter seemed, as I put it, 'a bit Irish'!

Danby, Loxton and Stott immediately replied to me in strong terms and threatened that, in the light of my letter, they were advising Sidney to withdraw from the transaction.

I telephoned Robert, who rang me back later to say that he had spoken to Sidney, and they were both quite agreed upon the area of land which was to be bought and sold.

'Have you said something to offend Sidney's solicitors?', Robert asked me.

It was only later when I looked rather more closely at Danby, Loxton and Stott's letter heading, at their list of partners and their reference on the file of correspondence, that I realised exactly where I had gone wrong.

The name of Sidney's solicitor was a Mr Seamus Flanagan.

There are two jobs in the garden to be done every August, neither of which are much fun. The first is to cut down the raspberry canes which have just fruited and tie in the new canes; and the second is to trim the privet hedge, which by this time of year is generally completely out of hand. Privet hedges have become rather unfashionable in recent years. I always reckon to be able to recognise gardens of a certain period by the presence not only of privet, but also of laurel and a few old nettle-smothered gooseberry bushes, whose best fruiting days have long since passed.

As I started to cut the hedge using hand shears, I disturbed several stick insects, which reminded me of the time our younger son Johnny proudly brought back one of these small creatures from school in a jam jar. He took great delight in furnishing the jar with sticks, foliage and a little water at the bottom for his pet to drink.

The following morning, Rosemary and I were awoken by shouts of dismay from the kitchen. We rushed downstairs to find that Johnny was standing by the jam jar and pointing at his pet stick insect, which appeared to be lying upside down and lifeless at the bottom of the jar.

'We may not be too late', I said to Rosemary with more hope than confidence, as I gently removed the creature with my pair of entomological forceps and laid it to rest on the table.

111

At this point Rosemary took over, and as she gently blew upon the prostrate insect, it slowly came to life. In a few minutes it had clearly made a miraculous recovery.

'I know you're a trained nurse, darling', I said to her, 'but I bet you never thought you'd ever have to give the kiss of life to a stick insect.'

Johnny's pet was eventually released into our privet hedge. I like to think that those I have just disturbed in the course of its annual trimming are its descendants.

I always wonder every year if I really dare leave the office to go on holiday with my family. This year we are going to Devon, but the problem is in actually getting away, for it is all such a last-minute panic both at home and at the office.

I hate the two or three days before and after a holiday. Each year I pray for an emergency-free period before leaving the office, just two or three nice and easy routine days. Somehow it never seems to happen.

This year, less than half an hour before my departure from the office, I received three telephone calls. The first was from a client wanting a power of attorney preparing immediately; the second was from another client who required me to take out an injunction against his neighbour for an alleged trespass; and the third was a particularly irate call from Chris Rawden, who had apparently made an arrangement with the couple buying his house that they would pay him £1,000 for all his carpets. This arrangement had been completely private, and neither solicitor had been informed. Chris was now phoning to say that the buyers had refused to pay for the carpets after the house keys had been handed over.

'You should have told me about this', I said, 'then we could have made sure it was in the contract.'

'I realise that now', replied Chris, 'but what do you suggest I do?'

'Have you a set of spare keys for the house?', I asked.

'Yes.'

'Well, I suggest you go straight back to your house and tell your purchasers politely but firmly that if you are not paid cash there and then, you will take up and remove all the carpets.'

'Is that legal?', asked Chris rather nervously.

'The time has come for practical action', I replied, showing that lawyers can be as adept as politicians when it comes to answering or rather not answering questions.

I left the office there and then, with the telephone still ringing.

We have at last got ourselves organised and away on our journey. It is comparatively easy to travel from Yorkshire to Devon, being motorway nearly the whole distance.

Although holiday journeys are undoubtedly quicker these days, they are, I think, considerably less interesting then those of my childhood. In those days the journey itself was very much part of the holiday. The one I remember best was not the short trip to Filey or Harwood Dale, but the longer one to Eastbourne, where my aunt and uncle ran a small hotel. This journey centred upon the A1, which I shall forever think of by its more romantic and traditional name of the Great North Road. I remember all its landmarks, especially its pubs and hostelries, the Boot and Shoe, the Brotherton Fox and the Punch at the northern end, and further south the Haycock and the Ramjam.

We generally had about four stops. The first somewhere near Newark for coffee and a quick game of football or 'catch' in a local park; the second for a picnic lunch near Huntingdon, where I tended to go off butterflying and be in danger of being left behind; the third break was always at Tilbury where we caught the ferry to Gravesend; and the final stop would be for a cup of tea in a Kent village, where one year there was the added pleasure of a cricket match to watch. Finally the glorious sight of the Sussex downs would come into view, and I would at once be dreaming of running across them with my butterfly net in pursuit of the elusive chalkhill and adonis blues.

This year our few days of holiday in North Devon have come and gone too quickly. We have been swimming a lot, played tennis, danced, putted, flown kites, or just walked and explored the Devon coastline. More importantly, we have talked and laughed and just been together as a family. It may be the last holiday of its kind, for our two eldest are now students and they will, I feel sure, wish to 'do their own thing' next year. Such family togetherness is precious and ought to be savoured.

On the journey back to Yorkshire, I was still quietly smiling to myself at a conversation I had overheard on our last day on the beach.

One man was talking to another, who was obviously a friend or relative.

'Where have you been all afternoon?'

His friend replied:

'I've been sitting on the cliff top.'

'What were you doing there?'

'I was contemplating the meaning of life.'

'Did you reach any conclusion?'

'I decided to go for a clotted cream tea', came back his friend's considered reply.

What a wise man, I thought to myself.

Back to the office, and I had hardly walked through the door when there was a telephone call from a lady who was in great distress because her only daughter had just, during a holiday in Turkey, married a citizen of that country whom she had known for only a matter of days. Was there anything to be done, what were her daughter's rights and what did I think about it all? My considered advice would have to wait, I told her, until I knew rather more about the circumstances and facts of the case.

I must confess that my immediate reaction was simply to be thankful that my own daughter had only gone on holiday as far as Devon this year.

Chapter Nine

'Lovely September, when the first leaves fell
and the first frosts came and folk said
"How the days are drawing in".'
                                    John Moore

On one of those golden but, alas, fast vanishing days of late summer
I was surveying my garden, and was pleased to see that there was
still quite a lot of colour in it. The fuschia by the summerhouse was
probably just at its best, the roses and honeysuckle were still in bloom,
whilst among the golden rods and michaelmas daisies there was a
steady hum from 'innumerable bees', and few late small tortoiseshell
and red admiral butterflies were settling on the flowers.

It was the sort of day when I was pottering rather than doing some
solid work. I happened to notice, in a rather weedy and neglected
corner of the garden, a few old pieces of wood, corrugated iron and
wire netting – which I suddenly realised were all that was left of a
den I had made for the children when they were quite small.

Somehow I always associate dens with early September, for it was
at the end of the long summer holidays when we children always
gathered in our favourite den for a last get-together and picnic before
going back to school. As my sister, cousins and any specially-invited
guests joined me in cramming into our secret hiding place, we never
wasted any time in demolishing the feast. The food consisted of crisps,
sandwiches, parkin provided by one of our mothers, and blackberries
which we picked from a nearby hedgerow. The drink was Tizer or
Dandelion and Burdock, and the weather on such occasions was
always perfect.

The dens we made were many and various. My cousin Robert was
undoubtedly the best amongst us at making them, for being a practical
chap, his dens were always painstakingly and solidly constructed with
posts and planks. His tree houses in particular were works of art, and
it would not surprise me if some are still standing to this day. By way

of complete contrast, I tended to favour more natural dens, situated either under the roots of an up-ended tree or at the back of a thick beech hedge, heavily camouflaged with foliage.

I rather think that anybody looking at the different ways Robert and I made dens could probably have predicted that Robert would become an engineer and I would become a country solicitor or even a writer! I certainly knew I would never become a builder.

I stood for a few minutes, looking wistfully at the pieces of wood and wire netting in my garden as I remembered the tremendous fun we all had as children when, during those long school holidays, we made dens, the sun was always shining and every day was summer.

'Where has childhood gone?', I asked myself as I walked back to the house. 'Why can't some things stay the same for ever?'

I once had a client called Gilbert Jones who had a most irritating habit of asking 'Are you with me, Mr Francis?' at regular intervals during the telling of his case, and invariably after the most simple statement on his part.

'I was catching the bus from Denley to Leeds', he told me on one occasion, 'when the bus set off before I was on properly. Are you with me, Mr Francis?'

Now, there are many people in this world who are a lot quicker on the ball than I, but I already felt to be several steps ahead of him. I just nodded as he continued.

'Well I lost my balance completely and fell down the aisle of the bus – are you with me?'

I nodded again and he went on.

'So there I was, lying on the floor, when the driver realised what had happened and put on his brakes – are you with me?'

By the time Gilbert had finished his story – which ended with the same question again – I had to resist saying that I had formed a very accurate picture of his case some time before he had finished speaking. I was still not altogether sure whether his oft-repeated question was just a nervous habit, or whether he genuinely believed his solicitor was a bit slow on the uptake.

There was a man who died earlier this month, a farmer called Ned Ripley, who reminded me of Gilbert Jones because he never seemed to understand what I was saying to him. Many a time I felt like asking him Gilbert's favourite question. There would be a puzzled, uncomprehending look on Ned's face as I explained the law to him on a particular subject, then repeated the explanation, repeated it yet again. Then, just as I would be about to give up and start asking myself whether my explanation was at fault, he would lean back, fold his hands together in front of him and say:

'Aye, Ah've grasped it.'

Ned was one of those farmers reluctant to put money into a bank or building society account, let alone in anything as daring as National Savings, unit trusts or equities. On more than one occasion, his accountant, Derek Bowers, and I spent some considerable time advising him about investments generally and on the sort of interest he could expect to receive. Ned looked at us as if this thing called 'interest' was just new to the Dales, but eventually he leaned back in his usual way and said to us both:

'Aye, Ah've grasped it.'

We were not altogether sure whether Ned had 'grasped it', but we were to find out. Ned had died suddenly, and Derek Bowers and myself, who were his executors, both received a telephone call from his local bank manager to say that in his vaults there was a security box belonging to Ned which he had given instructions should only be opened on his death. Derek and I went round to the bank, where the box was duly opened for our inspection.

Now very often security boxes in banks contain little more than bills, receipts and personal letters – but this time it was different. The box contained £50,000 in used notes, and nothing else.

'I can tell you that this box has not been touched for at least five years', said the bank manager.

I started to reckon up in my mind the huge amount of interest that Ned had lost on his money, but Derek – his accountant – was, I suspect, thinking of something entirely different, namely how he would explain this large amount of cash to the Inland Revenue.

Accountants are always worried when I tell them there is a security box at the bank belonging to one of their deceased clients. Such a box may contain no more than a collection of old bills and receipts, uncle Jack's gold watch and a few photographs and personal letters; or it may, as in Ned's case, contain a large amount of money hitherto unknown, impossible to account for and undeclared to the Inland Revenue.

'Ah well', I consoled myself, 'that's Derek's problem.'

I realised with a shock the other day that I had hardly been fishing at all this season. I couldn't see my way to taking any more time off from the office, but on arriving home in the evening it was warm and sunny, so I decided on the spur of the moment to get out my faithful old Hardy split cane fly rod, tackle up and walk down to the river for a spot of 'dapping' along the bank before supper.

'Dapping', which has always been considered, by most anglers at any rate, a perfectly legitimate form of fishing, consists of tying a very large bluebottle-type fly to your line and just dropping it into the river near to the bank in an effort to persuade any trout lying there that a 'goody' has just dropped off the overhanging branches.

Fly fishing on our local river is extremely difficult at the best of times, the banks being so tree-lined that it is dificult to cast a fly without the line becoming entangled in the branches. But I had noticed on a walk only the week before that there were several spots close to the banks where fish were rising, so I made for the first of these places quietly and carefully.

I crept up behind an alder tree, below which I knew there was a good trout pool, and dropped my fly into the water only a couple of

feet from the bank. There was a sudden splash and swirl, and I knew at once that my fly had been taken. I struck, but alas too soon and the fish was lost. I had simply not allowed enough time for the trout to take the fly down to the bottom.

'Bad luck, mister', shouted a lad whom I had not noticed before and who was fishing about twenty yards downstream.

He proudly showed me his catch, two splendid half pounders which he told me he had caught in the space of fifteen minutes. He had been float fishing using maggots as bait and told me he'd never seen 'dapping' before, so he asked if he could follow me to my next pool to watch what happened. This time I was successful, but the trout proved fractionally under the permitted size when I measured it.

'Can't you stretch it a bit, mister?', asked the lad.

I shook my head, and as I returned the fish to the river I thought it would never do for a solicitor who was a member of the local angling club to be caught breaking their rules by taking undersized trout from the river!

All fishermen like to be catching fish, but it is more important, I think, when you are young and have just taken up the sport than when you have been an angler for some years.

For my part I am happy just to be by a river, and catching fish certainly gives me no more pleasure than seeing a hatch of mayfly or catching a glimpse of a kingfisher.

Over the years I have had much pleasure from fishing and I hope there will be more in years to come, but no future experience is likely to equal the thrill of catching my first trout at Hayburn Wyke; or the very first time I went sea fishing off Eastbourne pier, when, to the consternation of all the old lads who had been fishing there all day without a bite, I hauled up a fine plaice with my very first cast. I carried the fish back to my aunt's hotel in triumph, where it was specially cooked by the chef and brought in to the dining room to the applause of the hotel residents.

My little 'dapping trip' did not result in a trout for supper, but I was not too downhearted and certainly not for long, for what sustains all anglers is partly the memory of past successes, but much more importantly the vision of that 'big 'un' you are always going to catch – 'next time'.

One of the problems when you have a busy office job is finding time to go to the dentist, the optician and the barber. A visit to the dentist is quite literally a pain, having one's eyes tested is necessary if boring, but going to my barber for a haircut is a pleasure. Early this month I realised that once again I was due for a trim.

In admitting that I dislike the modern 'unisex' hairdressers, I suppose that I must plead 'guilty' to what some would no doubt call typical male prejudice, but I have to say in all honesty that I go and will continue to go to a traditional gent's barber quite happily and without any guilt whatsoever!

Now traditional men's hairdressers, like traditional family solicitors, seem to be a dying breed, but there are thankfully one or two still left in the Dales. So it is to Arthur's shop that I go for my regular haircut, and where I can at the same time relax in a comfortable all-male atmosphere.

When I was a boy there were plenty of shops like Arthur's, all with their brightly-painted red and white barber's poles hanging outside, their floors full of different coloured hairs which were spasmodically swept away. They were establishments where the proprietors always seemed exceptionally well-informed about horse racing and where, in between giving hot tips on the likely winner of 'the 2.30 at York' to their older customers, they could be heard discreetly asking young men about to leave the shop after their haircut:

'And will there be anything else sir?'

We boys, who were probably more innocent than the present generation, nevertheless knew exactly what was implied in that question, and sniggered as we looked at certain advertisements in the shop and at certain products under the glass counter. The barber's question which interested us much more at that age, however, was the one which invariably came right at the end of the haircut:

'Would you like anything on, sir?'

What I really wanted to ask for at that stage was some Brylcreem, so that I could try to look like Dennis Comptom when I played cricket, but I was only allowed to ask for 'a little spray'.

I had to wait for the next school trip to the municipal swimming baths, where we boys used to fight each other to be the first to reach the 'Brylcreem machines' which doled out a much-prized 'wodge' of the stuff when you inserted a couple of pennies in them.

As a boy I hated having to wait at the barbers, but at Arthur's shop I am always more than happy to wait my turn. The shop itself is interesting, for apart from combs, brushes, scissors and shaving things, there are a number of different fishing rods and a fine selection of pipes. I immediately warm to any man who has the good sense to be both a fisherman and a pipe smoker!

Even more interesting than Arthur's shop are the customers attracted to it. Many are farmers and real Dales characters, and as I went into the shop for my haircut there was just such a customer getting into the barber's chair. Arthur, who knew him of old, asked him:

'How would you like it, Fred?'

'Less', was Fred's direct and economical reply.

There were two other farmers sitting next to me talking to each other, as we waited our turn. The subject under consideration by these two worthies was the fascinating one of how best a man could avoid doing the washing up. Billy reckoned that the easiest way was simply to tell the missus 'that 'e 'ad a poorly back', whilst Jack was equally sure that the safest method was 'to git right out o' t' road'.

Billy and Jack then got on to teasing Arthur about the very modest increase he had made for the price of a haircut, a price which had stayed the same for years and which even now is as cheap as any you can find in Yorkshire. The two farmers knew this perfectly well, but they nevertheless decided to make something of the price rise.

'How dus tha reckon tha'll manage wi' Arthur's new price?', Jack asked Billy.

'Nay, Jack, it's a beggar. But there's one thing Ah know, Ah'll not be tekkin' t' missus dancin' ivvery fortneet as we've dun in t' past.'

The two farmers turned to Arthur, and Billy said:

'Is there owt tha can do for us, like?'

Arthur laughed but said nothing. There was a short pause before Jack spoke again.

'Ah've jus' bethought misen, an' Ah reckon Ah've gitten t' answer to t' job.'

'Reight, Jack, well let's be knowin', like', said Billy impatiently.

'It's that simple lad, tha'll be fair capp'd tha nivver thought on it thisen', replied Jack.

'Cum on, let's be in on t' secret', said Billy, who was by now even more impatient.

At this point Arthur looked up again, and he and I were both by this time eager to hear Jack's solution to his friend's problem.

'Why', said Jack, in a tone of voice which implied that every man in the shop should have known the answer all along, 'Yer missus can pay for t' dancin', lad. Yer missus can pay!'

This is a satisfying month in the garden, the time of year when you enjoy the harvest of your hard work earlier in the season.

In the vegetable garden, there are potatoes in plenty, peas, beans, onions and some carrots – although not enough of them to store in sand, the method 'Owd Jacob' always taught me was the best for keeping them through the winter. I reflect once again as I bring all this produce to the kitchen that, although you may not save a lot of money growing your own vegetables, it is worth doing simply for the flavour, which is so much better than that of vegetables bought in the shops.

I have been particularly pleased that my parsley has done so well this year. It is always tricky to grow successfully from seed. 'Owd Jacob' reckoned you had a better chance chucking some seed over your shoulder rather than growing it in rows. I have always found that it helps if you pour freshly-boiled water along the drill before sowing. The seeds seem to germinate faster this way, and this year I have been rewarded by two particularly strong rows. I have not been slow in reminding Rosemary of the old country belief that when parsley grows well in a garden it is a sure sign that it is the wife who wears the trousers in the house!

This is the time of year when I always keep a sharp look out for field mushrooms, which ideally should be gathered on one of those magical misty mornings, taken straight to the kitchen and cooked for breakfast along with bacon, eggs and tomato.

Most toadstools, puffballs and fungi can be eaten, although I would not personally care to recommend any of them. Field mushrooms remain the real prize, but they are notoriously fickle in appearance.

I was so interested in them as a boy that I once bought some spawn out of my precious pocket money, and planted it carefully in various places under the lawns and rough grass. Being an impatient boy, I woke up next morning and looked out of my bedroom window, fully expecting to see mushrooms springing up all over the garden. Alas, there never were mushrooms in our garden, and I was equally disappointed when I tried growing them in a combination of loam and horse manure in our woodshed. I never seemed to get the temperature quite right. The huge crop I kept promising the family never materialised.

It is not every year that I manage to find field mushrooms, but I know an old Dalesman called Tommy Winters, who seems to gather baskets full of them every year.

'Where did you get them, Tommy?', I asked him in the pub one evening earlier this month.

'Wheer Ah allus gets 'em', was his classic Yorkshire reply.

Rosemary and I do not eat out very often at local pubs and restaurants; one of the main reasons being that I am in danger of meeting clients there, who more often than not will tackle me as to the progress of their particular case. Even when we have taken the precaution of going to an eating place far afield, thoughts of business can still intrude.

Earlier this month, we motored to a restaurant some distance from home for an evening meal. It was our first visit there, and we found upon entering the dining room that it was quite small and the tables were very close to each other.

Sitting at the table immediately to our right were a middle-aged man and a considerably younger woman, whose conversation we could not help but overhear. The subject under discussion was whether, and if so when, the man should leave his wife in order to set up home with his dining companion.

When eventually he said to his lady friend, 'My wife's already been to see a solicitor, you know', Rosemary leaned across our table and whispered some words to the effect that I might at this stage profitably pass my business card to him. I decided without too much difficulty to resist the temptation and to concentrate on the meal instead!

In a similar way, people who come to see me at my office sometimes find it hard to forget their own occupation, particularly if they are salesmen or dealers. We solicitors expect to receive calls from company reps hoping to sell us stationery, insurance, office equipment and sometimes rather more interesting products like wine and paintings, but when our clients try to sell things to us as well, then this solicitor at any rate finds his tolerance rather strained.

I have already had two people in my office this month who have tried to sell me insurance policies and other financial 'packages', but earlier this week I found myself involved in a new experience when someone actually tried to buy something from me.

My interview with Jimmy Knight had come to an end and I was showing him to the door, when he suddenly stopped and looked at a couple of old wooden chairs at the back of my office which had been there for as long as I could remember.

'I'll offer you £100 for each of those chairs', he said suddenly.

'£100 each? Really?', I replied, somewhat taken aback but trying desperately hard not to show it.

'Yes, Mr Francis, I'll pay you in cash now if you like', said Jimmy, taking out his wallet which was bulging with tenners.

I paused for a moment as I reflected that the two chairs in question, which I had never really noticed before in over twenty-five years at the office and which I certainly had never realised were of any value, were probably worth rather more than the amount Jimmy was so eager to pay in cash there and then.

I decided that I was not going to be rushed into anything, particularly as I remembered that Jimmy was a part-time antiques dealer.

'Well, Mr Knight, I think we'll just leave it for now, but I may get in touch with you if we have a bad year', I replied to Jimmy's obvious disappointment.

That great day in September has arrived at last when all roads lead to Denley for the occasion of its famous annual agricultural show.

There is a steady procession of cars, wagons, Land Rovers, trailers and all manner of farm vehicles along the narrow winding country roads leading from the moors, dales and fells of the surrounding area. There are not many folk who will be staying inside their cottages and in their grey stone villages this day.

I have been to a great many agricultural shows over the years and in many different places, but Denley Show is somehow special, because it combines the event of the year for the local farming community with a unique social occasion for Dalesfolk to meet, to reminisce, to renew friendships and to catch up with all the news and latest gossip.

On such an occasion, I cannot walk for more than a few yards without meeting friends and business acquaintances who more often than not want to remember times past.

'Na then, Mr Francis', said farmer Joe Stein, thumping my shoulder rather too heartily for comfort. 'Ah remembers when tha were nobbut a lad. Tha were allus laikin' i' muck.'

I laughed as I recalled the happy times I had spent at Joe's farm as a boy, helping with odd jobs on the land and playing there with other boys and girls from the village.

Rosemary, who understandably did not want to spend her day listening to me reminiscing, tugged my arm discreetly. We moved quickly on to the dog section, where it struck me yet again how uncannily some owners seem to resemble their pets.

Rosemary pointed out a rather formidable looking lady whose favourite expression, she recalled, was 'I'm feeling dogged up'. She never spoke a truer word, for the last time I accompanied Rosemary to her house, we had to share her tiny living room, where she served us coffee, with nine fully-grown great danes and three puppies!

We proceeded from the dog section quickly past the rabbit tent, where we spent an involuntary hour and a half last year during a sudden downpour; and on to the goat department, where we admired the sleek Saanens, the Toggenbergs with their floppy ears, and the handsome British Alpines, all reminding us of our own goat-keeping days.

We overheard a goat-keeping lady with white hair, pink cheeks and a very decided voice, warning a young woman in no uncertain terms against her idea of tethering her newly-acquired goats as opposed to keeping them free range.

'If it rains and you don't get them in immediately – and I mean immediately – you will have dead goats on your hands, my dear.'

In the cattle tent, as we stood among the fine Friesians and Herefords and watched the bulls being led out into the ring, Rosemary and I chuckled as we remembered the times when, with other village children, we spied on people from behind garden fences and hedges. If there was a woman in the garden we called out 'Hello, Mrs Bull', paused and then shouted 'Sorry, it's a cow', before running off. If there was a man in the garden, the shout would be, 'Hello, Mr Cow, sorry it's a bull'.

We looked fairly quickly at the pigs but rather longer at the sheep, the Mashams and Dalesbred, Blue-Faced Leicester, the huge Texels, the splendid Wensleydales with their thick shaggy coats, and we listened to the talk of the sheep farmers.

'Ow were t' lambin' this time?', asked one.

'None sae bad. There were a fair few gimmers, like', replied his friend. 'There were a case o' pulpy kidney disease ovver at Jim Dodson's place, tha knows, an' sum broxy t' other side o' t' dale. Ah reckons Ah were lucky.'

I knew that broxy came from sheep eating frosted grass, but I had to confess to Rosemary that I knew nothing of pulpy kidney disease. She laughed as she told me she had read in a book once that the first indication of the disease is a dead lamb!

At this point Rosemary and I went our separate ways. I walked over to watch the cricket, whilst Rosemary headed for the Womens

Institute exhibition, where several years ago she herself was awarded the coveted winning red ticket for a pressed flower picture.

After watching the cricket for a little while, I suddenly felt thirsty. As Rosemary was still obviously engrossed in the Womens Institute exhibition, I made my way towards the beer tent.

There were many familiar faces in the crowd around the bar. In the far corner I spotted those elusive brothers, Fred and Joe Westgate. They were drinking pints of ale and talking animatedly to their farming cronies.

Now was the time to get them together, I thought, and decided to seize my chance. I approached them quietly from behind and tapped them each on the shoulder.

'I've been trying to catch you two together all year', I said, as they turned round in surprise.

They recovered themselves quickly, and started playing their famous double act as if by instinct.

'Aye well, Mr Francis', said Joe, 'it dusn't do to be too 'asty wi' this soart o' job.'

'Joe's reight, tha knows', added Fred loudly as he emptied his beer glass. 'Na don't fret thisen, Mr Francis.'

As Fred ordered another pint, I anticipated that he was about to use his favourite expression. I was not disappointed.

'It'll be reight', he said.

With that, the two brothers resumed their conversation and their beer drinking.

As I finished my own beer and made my way out of the tent, still shaking my head, I was greeted by my old friends George and Elinor Dixon.

'Na then, Mr Francis, what would tha say to a glass o' whisky?', asked George with a wink and a mischievous smile.

'No thanks, George. I can't stop. I've just seen my wife coming out of the WI tent. Anyway, hadn't you better save it for cousin Joseph?', I replied with a laugh.

Rosemary and I joined up again to listen to the local brass band playing, and the strains of *Finlandia* followed us as we left the showground. A brass band playing such a tune has the same nostalgic and uplifting effect upon me as listening to a recording of Richard Tauber's *You are my heart's delight*, Gracie Fields singing *The Lord's Prayer* or of Paul Robeson singing practically anything.

126

Just as we reached the the exit gates, we heard a competitor in the vegetable produce section complaining bitterly to one of the judges about the result of the competition, in which much to his surprise and disgust he had found himself unplaced.

The judge in question, who was obviously an old hand at dealing with such a matter, met his complaint with a philosophical shrug of his shoulders and just one sentence:

'Well, Fred, Ah reckons it wouldn't do if we were all tae choose t' same lady!'

'Now that', as I remarked to my wife on our way home, 'is the truest thing I've heard all day!'

Chapter Ten

'Since golden October declined into sombre November
And the apples were gathered and stored . . . '
                                                    T S Eliot

It is still 'golden October', and I have just gathered the last of the
apples in my small orchard, apart from a few at the top of the trees
which I could not quite reach. How infuriating and frustrating it is
that the ones which are left for the wasps and the late autumn gales
are always the best.

At any rate the crop is gathered, and as I brought the last basketfull
into the kitchen I could not resist sampling one or two. Big boys,
as well as small boys, have long known the pleasure of eating
freshly-picked apples. Ovid, whose poetry I read and struggled to
translate when I learnt Latin at school, also knew the feeling:

'Et magis adducto pomum decerpere ramo
Quam de caelata sumere lance jubat.'

'It is more pleasing to pluck an apple from the branch which you
have seized than to take one up from a graven dish.'

I cannot for the life of me understand why so many Golden
Delicious apples are sold in England. This French imposter, whose
name surely comes close to contravening the Trade Descriptions
Act, does not in my opinion compare in any way with our own
native Cox's Orange Pippin, or, for that matter, with the splendid
James Grieves apples which I have just gathered in my own orchard,
and which with its pale green skin flecked and streaked with crimson,
is attractive in appearance, crisp to eat and fruits well even in our hardy
northern climate.

I read in the newspapers recently, as I seem to have done for years,
of the country's adverse trade balance. I may be naïve and an innocent

in economics, but it has always seemed to me that the remedy for this perennial problem lies not with politicians but with ourselves. If we all took the trouble to buy British products where available, we would surely not only retain and create employment for our people, but we would also reduce the trade deficit – and where better to start than by buying English apples when in season?

Whenever I have been working in the garden, I like to have a quiet walk around it, and on the very same day that I harvested the fruits of the orchard I was thrilled to see a covey of partridges in my field.

Now pheasants are quite regular visitors, often roosting up in our copper beech tree, but partridges are a rare sight. Their welcome presence in the sunshine reminded me of a snatch from a poem by Patrick Chalmers about 'Flickering, whickering partridges'. Unlike pheasants, partridges are monogamous, and I have always admired the efficient and and businesslike way in which they rear and look after their young.

Equally thrilling to see, just as I was about to come indoors for tea, was a number of goldfinches all busily pecking away among seeds of thistle heads in a neglected corner of my vegetable garden. Whoever invented the noun of assembly for these delightful little birds deserves to be congratulated, for 'a charm of goldfinches' is surely a perfect way of describing such a congregation.

The colours of a goldfinch, when seen at close quarters, are surprisingly bold and vivid, with the black and yellow wings, black and white tail, and black, white and crimson head and gorge; but as some sudden movement caused them all to fly off, all I could see as I made my way back to the house was a flash of gold as they all vanished from my garden and flew into the haze of the late afternoon sunshine.

It is generally around this time when I play my last tennis match of the season, before putting racquet and balls away until the following April.

'Why are you looking out of the window?', Rosemary asked me last Sunday morning.

'To see whether it's likely to stay fine for my tennis match', I replied.

It still makes me jump slightly whenever I am caught looking out of the window, because the very first time I was given detention at school was for committing that very crime – only on that occasion I was looking to see whether a cricket match was likely to be rained

129

off. During that first detention period, I was required to write an essay on a subject which my teacher said would test the power of my imagination:

'The inside of a table tennis ball.'

'When you have finished that essay', said my teacher, 'you can write another one entitled "The wages of sloth".'

It is, I think, the memory of struggling to compose those two essays which still makes me jump if anyone catches me staring out of a window.

Fortunately the weather held, and I travelled with the rest of the Denley team to Ghyllbeck Tennis Club to play our annual friendly match, the last fixture of the season.

I was thinking, as we journeyed up the dale, of all the jobs I should have been doing at home, and that I should really have gone to church, it being a Sunday. However, I remembered reading in a book written in 1881 by Lt Col R D Osborne:

'An afternoon spent at lawn tennis is a highly Christian and beneficent pastime.'

He also added memorably:

'Near at hand, under the cool shadow of a tree, there should be strawberries and cream and an iced claret mug.'

What a comforting and civilised prospect, and how pleasing to reflect that the very first person to devise a recognisable lawn tennis game was a solicitor called Harry Gem, who, with his friend Anguric Perera, founded a club at Leamington Spa for a game which they called 'Lawn Racquets'.

I was reflecting, too, on our journey up the dale about one of Wimbledon's early champions, a certain Reverend John Thorneycroft Hartley, Vicar of Burneston-in-Bedale and later honorary canon of Ripon, who dashed back to his Yorkshire parish to take Sunday service inbetween his Saturday semi-final and his Monday final. They don't breed vicars like that any more – not even in Yorkshire!

Hartley, a patient baseliner, would never have won Wimbledon in modern times, when a strong serve-and-volley game is essential for success. But he would, I am sure, have felt very much at home in our local league, where matches are often battles of attrition waged from the back of the court and where we, like Hartley, concentrate on keeping the ball in play and rely upon our opponents' mistakes.

Whether I was inspired by the memory of the illustrious tennis-playing parson or not I cannot say, but our match at Ghyllbeck ended in victory, a fitting end to the season. The memory of my inch-perfect lob volley which landed unplayably in the far corner of my opponents' tramlines, and which clinched the deciding rubber, will surely stay in my mind through the winter months – certainly long after I have forgotten all the double faults I served and the easy volleys I missed during the course of the season.

Last week, Rosemary and I were asked by one of our neighbours to keep an eye on his sheep whilst he was away for a couple of days. We have kept sheep of our own, but were still slightly apprehensive of the responsibility, for we remembered the time some bantams had been left in our care by another neighbour and one of them had died. Fortunately nothing went wrong with the sheep, but there are certainly dangers in such a situation. During my career as a solicitor I have seen litigation result from such arrangements.

I was consulted earlier in the year by a young woman called Jenny Frost who had been asked by her neighbour to look after their two dogs for a week whilst they visited relatives. Jenny had little previous experience of caring for dogs, but felt that she should be a good neighbour and comply with the request.

Unfortunately, on the very first day, the two dogs escaped from her garden, went straight into a farmer's field and started chasing sheep. The farmer, quite understandably, shot the dogs dead, and reported the incident to the police. The result was that Jenny not only had to break the news to her neighbours on their return, but also found herself facing a police prosecution because, although not the owner of the dogs, she was their 'keeper' at the relevant time.

A cautionary tale indeed, but by no means an isolated example of what can go wrong in such cases. Some years ago a client of mine, Miriam Oldbury, was asked to look after a neighbour's horse, which during the owner's absence on holiday developed certain serious problems. The vet advised immediate castration. His advice was accepted, but when the owner returned from holiday she was horrified, claimed she would never have consented to such a drastic operation and promptly sued Miriam for damages.

The case was so important to the parties that they were both represented by barristers at the subsequent trial. In the robing room, I overheard another barrister asking them what their case was about.

'Horse's balls', was the succinct reply they gave in unison.

131

Accidents which occur whilst looking after other people's animals can certainly have dire consequences, but there have been cases which have had their funny side.

A friend of mine, Leslie Butterworth, was once asked to look after a friend's pet hamster whilst he and his family went away on holiday. The hamster, which answered to the name of Paddington, did not take kindly to his new owner. On the second day, he bit Leslie's thumb very badly. Leslie was driven off immediately by his wife to the casualty department of the nearest hospital.

'What's happened?', asked the sister in charge.

'My husband has just been bitten by Paddington', replied Mrs Butterworth.

The sister turned on her heel, rushed out of the room and returned in a few minutes with the hospital's renowned senior consultant, Mr Mortimer Bailey, at her side. He came up to Leslie, who recognised the famous surgeon and said to him in a surprised tone of voice.

'It's really very good of you, but I didn't expect to be seen by a consultant for a little bite by a hamster.'

Mr Mortimer Bailey and the sister looked at each other for a moment, and then both burst into spontaneous laughter.

'Well, it may only be a small bite', said Leslie as he looked at his rather messy thumb, 'but I can't see that it's very funny.'

'I'm truly sorry, Mr Butterworth', replied Mr Bailey, 'but sister told me you'd been bitten by a bear from darkest Peru!'

I have spent much of my practising life acting for small shopkeepers. I have drawn up their leases, prepared their sale and purchase agreements, collected their debts, negotiated with their landlords, argued with the local council on their behalf, and generally advised them on the extraordinary range of problems which confront them in the running of their businesses.

It is with a genuine sense of regret that I have observed the disappearance of so many of them through changing social patterns, financial pressures and the advent of supermarkets.

This month I have seen two shops close in this way. As one by one the little shops of my Denley boyhood have disappeared, a part of me has died with them, for I grew up with them, knew them and loved them.

There are three particular kinds of shop which linger in the memory. Firstly the old-fashioned grocers shop, exemplified by

Fossets of Denley, with a large 'Provisions' sign outside, and inside a friendly shop assistant dressed in brown overalls and who always carried a pencil behind his ear. In such a shop, paper and string were used for wrapping, there were sacks of potatoes, a magnificent selection of cheeses, a large pair of scales, a marble counter and the smell of freshly-ground coffee.

The second type of shop I remember is the sweet shop, typified in Denley by Mrs Harbottle's little establishment just off the high street. I think that part of the fun in going there lay in deciding which of the varied and mouthwatering goodies on offer you would eventually choose. The choice was a difficult one. My own favourites were liquorice allsorts, Uncle Joe's mint balls, Fry's chocolate creams and Harrogate toffee. I could never resist buying a few hard-boiled sweets from the many different jars on the top shelf. They were real jaw-breakers, but they lasted for ever.

The third kind of shop which I shall forever associate with my boyhood was the one which had a sign outside it with the mysterious word 'Minerals' painted upon it. We children were never really sure exactly what the word meant, but we knew very well that whenever we stopped at such a shop during a bike ride, we would be able to buy ice cream, potato crisps and a bottle of pop.

It will be a sad day indeed if all the small shops go. Where on earth will folk then be able to buy the odd packet of nails, find a butcher to bone out a leg of lamb or just pop out for a packet of tea or loaf of bread when they run out? An even more important loss will be that of the personal touch. Where will people go to chat about the weather, the latest doings on the local council, or about who has just died, got married or had a baby?

A couple I saw earlier this month had tried and failed to run a clothes shop in Denley. Jayne and Peter Felgate had come to the town full of high hopes but, despite all their effort, hard work and obvious enthusiasm, the business had failed within a year.

They had probably judged their market incorrectly, for their clothes were probably too expensive for workaday Denley folk. In my experience, a farmer's wife who has decided to buy an expensive new dress is likely to make a day of it and buy in one of the big city centre shops.

The Felgates' shop, which had just closed, was at one time owned by one Stan Reed, a local Denley character, who was known for saying exactly what was on his mind to townsfolk and customers alike, no matter what their station in society might be. Stan's was a real old-fashioned haberdashers shop, and he carried an extensive and wide-ranging stock.

Locals still chuckle when they recall the story about 'a lady' newly arrived in Denley who visited his shop. Denley folk had already nicknamed her 'the model', because she looked and dressed 'a bit fancy' for their taste and 'talked lah-di-dah', as they put it. She certainly spoke with a refined accent and clearly had pretensions of grandeur. The locals knew very well that such 'airs and graces' were unjustified, as she was a nanny at one of the big houses.

'Now, Mr Reed', she said upon entering his shop, 'I wish to order a pair of stockings – but they must be gunmetal grey and of the very best quality.'

Stan, who had sized up his customer very quickly, said little but jotted down the order.

When 'the model' in due time called back to collect her order, she at once created an almighty fuss. Her raised voice could be heard not only by other customers in the shop, but by people standing halfway down the street.

'No!', she exclaimed in a loud and affected voice. 'No, Mr Reed, these stockings simply won't do. Can't you see that they are much too heavy and not the right quality at all – and just look at the colour, Mr Reed, that is not gunmetal grey.'

Stan, who had not said a word during this tirade, looked her straight in the face, put his pipe down on the counter and replied with a few choice words which caused his customer to flounce out of the shop.

'They're what we allus gets for t' likes o' you.'

There is an old legal joke about the lawyer who was asked to give an impromptu speech on the subject of 'Whisky and Water'.

'Sir', he said, 'it is an offence to make one in private and the other in public!'

I have not so far had occasion to defend anyone for distilling whisky in private, but earlier this month I was asked to represent Charlie Smith, a well-known customer in Denley pubs who had been summonsed to appear at the local magistrates court for urinating in public.

Charlie lives in one of Denley's typical stone-built terrace houses, two up and two down, with bathroom and lavatory downstairs.

Having retired to bed after drinking a fair amount of ale one Sunday lunchtime, and being too lazy to go downstairs to the lavatory, Charlie decided to relieve himself out of his bedroom window into the street below.

Now all might have been well if the coast had been clear, but unfortunately for Charlie, a lady pedestrian, dressed in all her finery after attending church for the morning service, chanced to come round the corner at that very moment and found herself in the direct line of fire. When she looked up and saw the cause of what had befallen her, she immediately and understandably rushed off to the police station in a state of extreme shock.

There really was no alternative for Charlie other than to plead guilty to the summons which inevitably followed. Trying to think of some meaningful mitigation to put before the court on his behalf was no easy task. As I racked my brains I remembered the words of a wise old Yorkshire solicitor who had once advised me:

'Remember, lad, however hopeless your case may seem to be, if you look hard enough and long enough, you should always be able to find something to say in mitigation on behalf of your client – even if it's only that he was born on Christmas Day with one leg six inches shorter than the other.'

In this case the only explanation Charlie could offer for having a pee *coram populo* as it were, was that it was an emergency, there were no stone walls handy, and as it was drizzling at the time he didn't think anyone would notice. In the event he was fined £25, which made it rather an expensive pee!

Thinking afterwards about Charlie's case reminded me of a time at school when I was struggling through a latin translation for my classics master, Canon Peachey.

Pointing his finger at me, he had said 'Come along, Fish Face' – for he invariably addressed his boys as either 'Fish Face' or 'Face Ache' – 'let's have some really fluent translation from you please'.

I made a hesitant start.

'Come along, we haven't got all day and you want to play cricket this afternoon, don't you? Now how many times do I have to tell you – subject, verb, object.'

I tried again.

'And . . . er . . . Zeus . . . er . . . made . . . er . . . water.'

135

At this point Canon Peachey, who had a fine sense of humour, looked at me gravely but with a twinkle in his eye as the whole class rocked with laughter.

'Literally a correct translation, Francis', he said, 'but you really have a most unfortunate way of putting it.'

There are surely few sadder sights in the countryside than that of a well-known and well-loved family farm going steadily downhill.

Reg Farndale and his wife Nora had struggled for years to make a go of the Dales farm they took on after the death of Reg's father. For a start, the farm was not quite big enough to be economically viable, and most of the fields consisted of rather poor 'outcrop' land bordering on the moors.

Even if other circumstances had been favourable they would have struggled to survive, but as it was they seemed to be struck by a never-ending sequence of disasters. In their very first winter, they lost their entire stock of winter hay when a barn burnt down; two years later, they had to rebuild their herd of cows from scratch following an outbreak of foot and mouth disease; and the year after that, Reg could not work for some months following an accident in which his tractor turned over.

There always seemed to be a crisis at Moor Top Farm and, despite their working long hours seven days a week, Reg and Norah were under constant pressure from their bank manager.

If their accountant and I had been honest with them, we would have told them both years ago that they would be much better off financially by selling up, paying off their debts, investing the balance and buying a little bungalow somewhere. I knew very well, however, that to give such advice would be a waste of time. Farming was in their blood – a way of life – and that without it they would be totally lost.

Despite all their misfortunes, crises and financial pressures, Reg and Nora remained stubbornly optimistic for many years.

'Summat'll turn up', was Reg's standard reply whenever his bank manager or accountant warned him about his hopeless financial position.

He always reminded me of a latter-day Mr Micawber, or of Billy Bunter waiting for the long-awaited postal order to arrive.

Earlier in the year the crunch finally came. Reg and Nora were forced into bankruptcy by their bank and other creditors. They left

the little farm they had loved and worked on for so many years, and as I said farewell to them I shuddered at their chances of making a new life for themselves.

On a dark windy day towards the end of the month, I passed their farm gate as I journeyed up their road. On impulse I stopped my car and stood for a few minutes looking across at the deserted fields. Moor Top Farm had not yet been sold. How quickly, I reflected, can a farm go to rack and ruin. I thought, too, of the haunting and melancholy lines of Hilaire Belloc:

'Hannaker Hill is in desolation
Ruin a-top and a field unploughed.'

I remembered the years of struggle for Reg and Nora – and of his parents before them – of all their hard work and of the laughter of their children when they were young and helped on the farm. It was all gone now, and the whole place was strangely silent.

As I turned back towards my car, dark clouds swept across from the moor and a sudden shower came out of the sky. I recalled in my sadness two more lines from the same poem by Belloc which seemed to express my feelings exactly:

'Spirits that loved her calling aloud
Spirits abroad in a windy cloud.'

A farmer very different to Reg Farndale was waiting to see me when I arrived back at the office after my visit to Moor Top Farm.

'You won't believe this, Mr Francis, but Jack Higgins is here again', said my secretary Clare as she greeted me.

I groaned inwardly and slumped into my chair.

'You had better show him in, I suppose', I replied, with as much enthusiasm as I could muster. Solicitors cannot pick and choose their clients after all.

Jack was never one to waste any time on pleasantries.

'Na then, Mr Francis, tha were a bloody dead loss ovver t' accident job, an' wi' t' bother ovver t' kitchen table.'

I realised even more strongly than ever, whilst Jack was talking, why they called him an 'ockard old bugger' up the dale, but I just swallowed hard and replied in my coolest professional manner.

'I'm sorry you're dissatisfied, Mr Higgins, but I have to advise on the law and this sometimes means telling people what they don't want to hear . . . '

'Aye well', interrupted Jack, 'it's all watter under t' bridge. Ah'm on wi' another job now.'

'What's that?', I asked.

'Well, it were seven month ago last Tuesday ah lent me nephew Jim fifty pund. 'E were skint at t' time, an' were short on a pair o' boots 'e needed to cum an' do sum work for us, like.'

'Has he paid you back?', I asked, as I guessed what was coming next. I guessed wrong.

'Oh aye.'

'Well, what's the problem then?'

"E were a month ovverdue wi' payin' me back. Sae what Ah wants to know is, what about t' interest?'

138

'Interest, Mr Higgins, you're wanting to claim interest on a fifty pound loan to your own nephew?', I asked incredulously.

'Well, Ah know it's not much . . . '

'You're right, Mr Higgins, it's absolute peanuts.'

'Ah knows that, but that's not t' bloody point', replied Jack, who was now starting to raise his voice. 'It's t' principle, like. Sae answer my question, am Ah entitled to interest?'

'Not unless Jim agreed to pay it when the loan was agreed.'

'Well, that doesn't seem reight when 'e were a month ovverdue', insisted Jack.

'I've given you my opinion, Mr Higgins', I replied, at the same time as I struggled to keep my non-legal opinions to myself.

Only a solicitor knows how incredibly mean, unreasonable and plain awkward some people can be.

'Ah nivver seem to git anywhere at this place', thundered Jack.

'You are perfectly free to consult another solicitor', I replied, fervently hoping that he would take up my suggestion.

'Ah might jus' do that', said Jack as he stormed out of my office – and not for the first time this year.

Jack may go elsewhere for his next case, but experience tells me that when you want a particular client to go, he never does. I suspect that with Jack it's a case of 'better the devil you know'.

'How did you get on?', asked Clare after Jack had left.

'Don't ask', I replied wearily, 'just don't ask.'

St Luke's little summer has been and gone, and on the very last day of the month the garden seemed a desolate and forlorn place. It is always a melancholy day in the gardener's year when you sweep up leaves for the first time and mow the lawns for the last time.

It is also the time of year when I aim to make a start on the winter digging. Of all the many different jobs there are to do in the garden, digging, I have always found, is perhaps the most satisfying of all. 'Owd Jacob' taught me that it is a job which should be tackled at a steady pace, neither too fast nor too slow and with plenty of pauses. You always know come the spring whether you have done it properly, for if you have, the winter frosts will have penetrated the large clumps of soil which you have turned over, and they will be easy to break down into a nice 'friable' loam.

It feels grand after half a day's digging to stand back for a little while, light a pipe, watch a robin alight next to the spade to feast

upon uncovered worms, and look with satisfaction upon an expanse of black soil neatly turned over. I imagine that a farmer experiences the same kind of pleasure in looking at a well-ploughed field.

It is good, too, at digging time to take a lump of soil in your hands and dissolve it through your fingers. Whenever I do this, I think of the famous soldier-poet Edward Thomas and of the occasion when he was asked by a friend why he was going off to fight in the First World War. Thomas bent down, picked up a handful of earth in his hands and replied: 'Literally, for this'.

His patriotism was not of the flagwaving, jingoistic variety, but was born out of his love of the English countryside, her people, her pubs, her customs and traditions, her way of life and of the very soil upon which he stood.

As I returned to the house, I noticed that the leaves on the trees up the dale were all gold, red and yellow, and the hedges were hung with berries. I saw, too, that there were still some blackberries left on the canes which grow around the garden walls, but being mindful of the old saying that 'he who picks blackberries in October picks them for the Devil', I passed them by. I am not by nature a superstitious person, but neither do I believe in tempting fate.

Rosemary reminded me over tea that it was Hallowe'en, the Eve of All Hallows, when in older times people lit fires to keep witches, devils and hobgoblins at bay.

We no longer roast chestnuts or play 'ducking for apples' as we did when the children were younger, but we still light turnip lanterns, messy and time-consuming to prepare, but worth all the effort when their ghostly yet comforting light, spreading from our bedside tables, sees us all safely through the night.

Chapter Eleven

'No sun, no shine, no butterflies, no bees
No fruits, no flowers, no leaves, no birds – November.'
Thomas Hood

Only two weeks ago I was standing at the garden gate on a still frosty morning, thinking of another memorable line from the same poet:

'I saw old Autumn in the misty morn – listening to silence.'

Now autumn has changed almost imperceptibly into winter, there is a wild west wind blowing, and the fallen leaves swirl around and chase each other down the drive.

It has been a ritual for as long as I can remember in our family at this time of year for each of us to catch a falling leaf and make a wish, by no means an easy task in a strong wind, but one which must be completed once you have set your mind to it, no matter how long it takes.

When I was a schoolboy, the beginning of November marked the end of the conker season, as we turned from horse chestnuts to the sweet chestnuts we roasted on Bonfire Night.

I still cannot resist chestnuts of either variety. There is something eternally magical in finding a large, shiny, polished mahogany-brown conker, but we schoolboys knew that it was not the biggest which proved the best in combat, nor the smallest, but it was the rather nondescript-looking medium-sized one which became the 'fiftier' and the envy of the class. As for sweet chestnuts, they are quite delicious, especially so when roasted in your own bonfire on Bonfire Night.

The conker season ended at the start of November, because our minds then turned to Mischief Night and Bonfire Night. Throughout the country, children and adults alike remember the fifth of November; but so far as I know, Mischief Night, celebrated the evening before, is a peculiarly Yorkshire tradition, possibly because of Guy Fawkes' connection with the county.

The Mischief Night trick most favoured by me and my friends was to creep up to a house, remove the dustbin lid, prop it up against the front door, ring the bell and finally run away to hide at a safe distance and watch to see the reaction when the door was opened.

I still feel guilty when I remember the time the door was opened by a lovely young lady who was dressed in a ballgown and elegant new party shoes. The heavy, rather dirty dustbin lid fell on those shoes, and from her anguished cries and from the irate shouts of her father, who had presumably paid for them, it was clear to us that they had been badly damaged. Her father ran after us but he was not fast enough to catch us!

On the day after Bonfire Night, as I picked up the remains of the fireworks we had let off and spread the ashes from the bonfire around my gooseberry bushes, I felt a distinct nip in the air, and noticed that the weather vane on the church tower had turned north. I wondered whether it would freeze sufficiently hard for Dalesfolk to be able to predict a mild winter:

'If there's ice in November to bear a duck
Then for t' rest o' t' winter, there'll be nowt but slush and muck.'

I sometimes wonder who on earth first thought up such sayings, for these two lines do not scan too happily, nor in all honesty have I ever found them to be true!

I am never happier in my job than when I am in the company of one of my old farming clients, listening to talk of life in the countryside in the old days.

Whether they were 'the good old days' or not is a matter of opinion, depending on which old farmer is doing the talking. Some reckon 't' ould days were t' best', whilst others tell me that the good old days 'weren't that good'. As with most such arguments, the truth probably lies somewhere between the two extreme views. One thing is for certain, there never was an idyllic golden age in the countryside, and the majority of our rural forebears undoubtedly led lives which were harder, poorer and shorter than our own.

I was reflecting on these matters as I drove to Grange Bottom Farm during the week after Bonfire Night to see one of my favourite clients, William Noble, who at the age of eighty-five still helps his two sons around the farm every day.

I used to visit Grange Bottom Farm when I was a boy, and the very first time I met William was when I went to explore one of his barns and found him sitting on a bale of straw. He appeared to be drilling holes in a wooden wheel ready for the spokes to be inserted. Being an inquisitive schoolboy, I asked him how he measured the distance between the holes to make sure they were the same.

'Reckovee, lad, reckovee', he replied.

I did not like to admit that I did not understand him, and it was some little time later that I discovered that his measuring was done by 'the reckoning of the eye'.

William invited me into his farm kitchen and, after we had concluded the business which was the reason for my visit, he was soon talking to me about the old days and of the many changes he had seen on the farm during his lifetime.

'Aye, it were good goin' i' them days for a man tae milk twenty cows a day. Ah've seen t' fashion change frae Irish heifers to British Friesians, 'ay to silage, an' 'osses tae tractors. Speakin' o' 'osses, there were a feller used to cum all round t' dale wi' a travellin' stallion.'

William paused for a moment and shook his head slightly before continuing.

'That were a tricky job, Ah can tell thee. It were reet enuff if t' mare were i' season, like, but if 'appen she weren't, there were all 'ell let loose an' t' stallion could be damaged wi' t' kickin' 'e'd gitten.'

William paused again, but only for a moment before changing the subject.

'Aye, lad, it were a big day when we changed ovver frae 'osses tae tractors. Them fust tractors weren't in t' same class as t' ones yer see on t' farm today, yet Ah felt even i' them days as if Ah were drivin' a Rolls Royce.'

I never interrupt William until he has finished talking, because every time he speaks I learn something about farming just by listening.

I have also learnt some good Yorkshire expressions from him over the years. 'Reckovee' was the first such word he taught me. Many others were to follow, but one of his favourites, which always stays in my mind, is 'afterwit'. If someone had made a comment to which he could only think of a witty rejoinder a day or so later, he used to complain to me that he had been 'troubled wi' afterwit'.

I was thinking about that as he showed me to the door, looked at my rather ordinary car and said, as farmers seem to enjoy saying to their solicitors:

'Ah reckoned tha'd be in a Rolls Royce!'

The reply I should have made, but did not think of until I got back to the ofice, was:

'But I'm not a farmer.'

I now know exactly what it feels like to be 'troubled wi' afterwit'.

A great deal of money is often made by disreputable dealers out of the disposal of the personal possessions of the deceased, simply because their executors do not always have any appreciation of their value. I have known this to be true for many years, and I was aware of it again just the other day when someone who was about dispose of a large collection of books suddenly remembered that I was interested in the subject, and asked for my advice.

When I had looked them over, I advised that the splendid collection of old angling and golfing books should be put into specialist sales, and the rest of the collection offered to the owner of a local secondhand bookshop whom I knew to be reputable.

It is a sad fact that many people believe books to be worthless, with the result that they are often given away or even tipped on the council rubbish dump. I was told recently by a book dealer that, upon hearing that some books had been disposed of in this way, he rushed up to the tip only to find that he was too late. A fine collection of early illustrated children's books had been irreparably damaged by rain. What a tragedy, what a waste!

I suppose that it is partly because so many people do not know the value of books that there is always the chance of finding a bargain at a church bazaar, an Oxfam shop, a jumble or car boot sale, or even at a catalogue sale.

I love to go to such events when I have the chance, even if it does mean spending a lot time on my hands and knees working painstakingly through the 'boxed' lots. It is, I think, the thrill of the chase which is the attraction, every bit as much as chancing upon a rare book for ten or twenty pence.

'Chancing upon' is surely the right description, for you never know what you are going to find at such sales. It is the proverbial lucky dip in the old bran tub. There are always many books which you cannot imagine anybody wishing to own – old hymn books, badly-damaged copies of books by long-forgotten novelists, plenty of examples of what used to be called 'temperance trash' and lots of scribbled-over children's annuals.

I always smile when I look inside a book and see written there after the name and address of the owner:

'Yorkshire
England
Europe
The World
The Universe.'

I immediately conclude that the book must have belonged to a contemporary, for children of my generation always inscribed books in that way.

You need to be very patient if you are a book collector, and it often happens that the best finds are made just at the moment you least expect them. For among the old hymn books, dated travel books and tatty paperbacks, you may just possibly find a first edition in fine dustwrapper of an early book written by a famous and highly collectable author.

Earlier in the year, a friend of mine found one of the early 'William' books, a nice first edition in a dust jacket, for just £8 in a car boot sale. He thought he had done rather vulgarly well when he resold it to a dealer for £150, but the self-satisfied smile disappeared from his face when he later learnt that the dealer had advertised the same book in his catalogue for £300!

My friend at the local bookshop has, in his despair and frustration, recently written to all local solicitors, asking them to remember him whenever they come across a collection of books in an estate, but I strongly suspect that many valuable libraries will continue to be lost because relatives, who know nothing of their possible value, will simply say:

'They're just a lot of old books, let's get rid of them.'

I have just been sampling the home-made beer which occupied our elder son during his long summer vacation. It went down reasonably well, but was a little too 'yeasty' for my taste and probably needs keeping for a while longer. In the meantime, I am hoping that Rosemary will soon allow me to be let loose upon her bramble and elderberry wine.

Beer and wine making are agreable hobbies for country people, and I know a number of people who are – if anything – over-enthusiastic in their invitations to me to taste their products.

The trouble with home-made wines is that, not only are they without exception extremely potent, but also after the first two or three glasses it is in my experience quite impossible to appreciate the difference between them. Potato, parsnip, gooseberry or whatever – they all eventually seem to taste exactly the same!

My former senior partner Phillip Lytton always made excellent beers and wines. He was not quite so successful, however, when he tried growing his own tobacco. In this country it is difficult to dry, a fact which became obvious when I used up a whole box of matches in trying to keep a single pipeful of Phillip's tobacco alight. I had thought of having a go at growing the stuff myself, but I have concluded rather sadly that our climate simply does not lend itself to tobacco growing.

Phillip regularly had jars of home-made wine fermenting in various rooms at the office, and on one unforgettable occasion I came within an ace of making a very serious mistake. I had gone into the office library with a view to looking up a case in the *All England Law Reports*, when I noticed a small bottle of what appeared to be a fairly light-coloured wine on the table. I was about to have a swig of it when Phillip happened to come into the room in search of a book. He saw me with the bottle in my hand, and a broad smile spread across his face.

'I wouldn't drink that if I were you, John.'

I looked at him in surprise.

'Isn't it a very good vintage?', I asked.

'Oh yes. That bottle contains a urine sample from a client of mine who was breathalysed last night', replied Phillip as he broke into a laugh.

Ever since that dreadful moment I have always tended to be rather cautious when offered home-made wines, unless I know exactly what they are and who has made them!

My 'gumboot practice' has been in full swing throughout the year, and this month particularly I seem to have spent more time seeing farmers than all my other clients put together.

Yesterday I journeyed a little way down the dale to see Jack Falshaw in order to discuss the terms of his proposed new will.

Now Jack is a dairy farmer and a noted local naturalist, perhaps best known amongst Dalesfolk for his unerring ability to tell the age of a tree at a single glance. He once surprised me in this fashion on an occasion when we were travelling down the farm lane in his old van to look at some outbuildings

'See that sycamore yonder, Mr Francis.'

I nodded as he pointed his finger, and I looked at the large tree which stood a good hundred yards away on my nearside.

'Ah've nivver looked at t' trunk close up, like, but Ah'll not be sae far out if Ah tells thee it's an 'undred an' forty year old.'

I looked at him in amazement, because it is not considered possible to determine the exact age of a tree without cutting it down so that all its annual rings can be counted on its stump. I knew, however, that a reasonably accurate estimate can be made by assuming an average rate of growth in girth for the kind of tree and the district concerned, such growth rates being expressed as 'annual rings per inch of radius'. But here was Jack telling me the age of a tree at a glance.

'How can you tell?', I asked him.

'Well, Ah worked i' forestry for a few years afore me father died an' Ah took ovver t' farm. When tha's bin wi' trees, tha soon gits tae know 'em.'

I suppose that Jack's unique ability to tell the age of a tree at a glance is based partly on that, partly on his local knowledge and partly on what fellow farmer William Noble simply calls 'reckovee'.

Jack and I have been firm friends ever since the occasion some years ago when I defended him at Denley magistrates court, where he had been summoned to appear for having, as the prosecution termed it, 'extraneous water' in his milk. It was, as local farmers would have called it, 'a milk-watterin' job'.

Jack could not explain the presence of water in his milk. He was, I knew, an honest man who would not dream of watering his milk deliberately to increase output; yet, as we both also knew, this would be precisely what the court would conclude had happened, unless we could provide a convincing explanation.

I had asked Jack to show me his entire production system, from the milking machines to the bottling. When he came to explain the cooling system, I had a sudden thought.

'Could your cooling system possibly be leaky?'

Subsequent tests by an expert proved that it was, much to Jack's surprise as well as relief that the answers to the puzzle had been found. The same expert gave evidence in court, which completely satisfied the magistrates as to the reason for there being 'extraneous water' in Jack's milk.

Other farmers up and down the dale were not so easily convinced, however. For years afterwards, whenever I visited a farmer in Jack's area, his first words to me, said with a smile and a wink would always be:

'Na then, Mr Francis, 'as tha cum across any o' them leaky coolers lately?'

Yesterday, as I returned home from the office, I was not sure whether to laugh or cry, for there had been incidents at work to provoke both reactions.

The day had started unpromisingly. My car had broken down on the moors above Denley, I was late for work, and by the time I had arrived at the office my first client was waiting to see me, so I had no time to sort through my large pile of mail or start my first batch of dictation.

The man who was waiting to see me was not about to improve either my mood or my temper. James Smith, a fussy little man who always seems to have files on every aspect of his business and personal life immaculately collated and transported in a large black briefcase, had been thinking over the advice I had given him a week earlier regarding a claim he was making as a result of a very minor road traffic accident.

'I have a friend who thinks you're going about my case the wrong way, Mr Francis – and a man I met in my club last night told me

I should be getting a lot more money from the insurance company than you've advised me to accept.'

I sat in my chair, inwardly fuming but just managed to control myself.

'My advice stands, Mr Smith, but if you have a friend who thinks he can do a better job for you than I can, then by all means ask him to represent you', I said rather icily.

I do not like losing clients, but with ones like James Smith, who are forever quoting the opinion of friends, barrack-room lawyers and people they have met in the pub, you can surely never win.

I sometimes think the public would be better served if the disastrous results of home-made legal deals, based on the advice of non-legally qualified friends, could be more widely publicised.

A few years ago, a farmer in a remote part of the Dales agreed to sell part of his farm to a neighbour. No lawyers were instructed and no deeds were drawn up, there was simply a handshake and a handing over of cash. They had been told by a mutual friend that they could save a lot of money if they did without a lawyer. A year later, the two farmers fell out and it took lawyers three years and a long court case to resolve matters.

If I were to look at the problem from another and perhaps rather cynical point of view, it is arguable that lawyers should encourage more 'DIY', because the lawyers will then have a field day in clearing up the resultant messes!

I was still feeling cross about James Smith when, as often happens at such times, I received a telephone call which made me laugh. Bill Farsley had just sold his house to a lady who lived in the same road. Because her own house had gas, she assumed that Bill's house just fifty yards away would also be suppplied. Upon completion she discovered that there was no gas connected, and she sought through her solicitors to obtain a last-minute reduction in price.

I couldn't help laughing as the sad tale unfolded from the lady's solicitor. It was a classic case of *caveat emptor* – 'let the buyer beware' – so I said:

'I'm really sorry, but she really ought to have checked to see whether there was any gas or not before she signed the contract.'

It never ceases to amaze me how casual some people are about important things when they are buying a house. They can, for instance, often seem far more concerned about the number and position of power points, or whether items of furniture can go in particular places, than the availability of mains services or the condition of the roof!

As I travel around the Dales villages, I cannot help but notice that many of them, particularly lower down the Dales, have changed in character over the years. Many of the housing developments are sadly out of keeping, and in some places there are hardly any locals left. Commuters and 'off cum'd 'uns' have replaced the sons and daughters of the original inhabitants who, unable to find jobs or afford housing in their village, have left long ago.

In many other villages, however, there is a good balance between locals and newcomers. As long as the latter do not try to make the former conform to the tidy suburban lifestyle from which they, the newcomers, have sought to escape, then the balance is a healthy one.

A village without newcomers is likely to be an insular, narrow-minded place. 'Off cum'd 'uns' often bring new life, new ideas and commitment to the church, the dramatic society, the village hall and to social life generally. What is more, if they treat the locals sincerely and without being patronising or condescending, they will themselves not only be accepted but will find true friendship.

Locals are often amazed at the sheer extravagance of many of those who move into the Dales and 'do up' their farmhouses and cottages. Huge sums are spent on new bathrooms, kitchens and extensions. 'They've more brass than sense' is an oft-heard comment in the pubs.

At the same time, such expenditure greatly benefits the local tradesmen, the builders, plumbers, joiners and wallers. At a time when some of the old Dales crafts are dying out, I strongly suspect that the small-time builders and wallers are doing far better than ever their fathers and grandfathers did.

As a gardener I am constantly surprised at the amount some folk will spend on landscaping work. I once had a client called Eric Stone, who moved from the outskirts of Leeds to a country property, where he decided to have the grounds professionally landscaped. He spent no less that £3,000 on the best quality Cumberland sea-washed turf.

The very day after the turf had been laid, some cows got into his garden during a thunderstorm. I could have wept for Eric when I inspected what had been his lawn, trampled by the cows into a muddy morass. I could have told him, however, if I had been asked, that if you choose to have a country garden then you must expect it to be visited by sheep and cattle from time to time, unless you take the most careful and elaborate precautions.

If you manage to keep the sheep and cattle out, that will not be the end of your problems. I have tried to keep rabbits and moles out of my garden for years. I have never succeeded and I surely never will.

I have often wondered what some of the Dalespeople themselves think about the physical changes to their villages and to the influx of 'off cum'd 'uns'. Earlier this month I had an insight into the thinking of one old Dalesman. After his death I went through his papers and personal effects. At the very bottom of his deeds box there was a piece of yellowy paper, upon which was written an extract from an anonymous poem, lines which clearly expressed his own feelings:

'Strangers'll come an bi takin' oor places,
Hardlins tha'll care as oor fore-elders er
For those tha'ed talked wi' an' kenned fra bein' childer
Who wrought all around an' luv ti them ger.

A few o' years pass, will t' oad name bi forgotten
Will t' lasses an' lads bi nobbut a tale.
Bud sum'll think on, whale life is within 'em
Warm hearts an' true, you can find in oor dale.'

I finished the month as I started it, by visiting a farming client. As I arrived, I found Sam Bates struggling with the jobs he had hoped to finish in the month. The land was heavy and wet, and he had obviously just brought his cattle into the half-covered stockyard where they could shelter from the worst of the weather.

Farmers and farm-workers have healthy appetites which come from hard physical work in the fresh air, and it is a good job that many of them have wives who know how to put on a good meal.

'You'll 'ave summat tae eat, Mr Francis?', said Sam, as he closed the stockyard gate and beckoned me towards the farmhouse. 'Our Doreen's just med us sum tea.'

Sam's invitation was given in a tone of voice which clearly would not take 'no' for an answer.

Now Sam loved his food and he never seemed to mind what it was – as long as there was plenty of it. He and his wife had a little ritual every mealtime. Doreen would offer him a choice of food and he would invariably reply, 'Ah'm not reet fussy, lass', or by way of variation, 'Ah'm not a reet proud chap'. He would then proceed to demolish everything laid before him with great relish.

As I looked at the huge bowl of Lancashire hotpot, the plate of scones, and the pies, cakes and cheeses, I took a deep breath, and as I tucked in I remembered the old Yorkshire grace:

'God bless us all an mek us able
To eat all t' stuff what's on this table.'

Chapter Twelve

'In a drear-nighted December,
Too happy, happy tree.
Thy branches ne'er remember
Their green felicity.'
John Keats

I make no apology for beginning the last as well as the first chapter of this book with a quotation from the same poet, for Keats is so often both accurate and evocative in his choice of adjectives.

The evenings of December are 'drear' indeed, and as I threw another log on the fire and drew the curtains to shut out the wind, rain and murky darkness, my mood of melancholy, which had started to set in during an afternoon walk, enveloped my thoughts.

It was a wild Saturday afternoon, the first of the month, when I put on boots and anorak and headed off towards the river, hoping that the accumulated cobwebs of a week's work would be blown away and my spirits uplifted.

When I was a pupil at Rossall we regularly gave thanks to the Almighty in the school chapel for, amongst many other apparent blessings, 'bracing wind and quickening rain', not uncommon features of the weather on the exposed Fylde coast – nor for that matter in the Yorkshire Dales. As I walked, head down, wet, wind-blown and miserable, across the fields to the river, it was not, I must confess, with a feeling of thankfulness in my heart.

When at last I reached the shelter of trees and started to walk along the riverbank, I saw a mink in the water, a sight which only served to increase my depression, for mink are born killers and whenever they appear, so river birds like moorhens disappear.

I have noticed, during the year, other changes in the river which are equally worrying. The switch by so many farmers from hay to silage has undoubtedly led to increased pollution, and the sheer volume of effluent from the growing number of fish farms must also be taking

153

its toll. Where there is over-intensive farming of any kind, disease will surely follow.

Even more worrying is the effect of upland drainage schemes. These have led to the river rising and falling more quickly than used to be the case, leaving it acutely vulnerable to periods of drought.

If the dippers disappear, I thought to myself, as I stood next to a waterfall feeling thoroughly despondent and soaked to the skin, then my worries really will reach a climax, for their presence is surely the litmus test of a healthy river.

I was still thinking about all these depressing matters in the evening, as I settled in my armchair and listened to the wild wind howling around the house and the rain beating upon the windows. I looked up at my bookshelves, and for some reason my eyes lighted upon my old school copy of Caesar's *Gallic Wars*. I suddenly remembered one word, *hibernaculu*, which cropped up regularly in those pages whenever Julius Caesar led his army 'into winter quarters' at the onset of winter.

I never succeeded as a schoolboy in working up any great enthusiasm for the lengthy accounts of Roman military campaigns and of troops laying waste to the countryside. I am sure I found the way armies passed their winters extremely boring, but in my present depressed mood I suddenly felt envious of those soldiers as I pictured them comfortably billeted in winter quarters, resting and slumbering away, no doubt fortified from time to time by wine, women and song, and enjoying the camaraderie of army life, until the days lengthened, the first sunny days of spring arrived and they all marched out once again to do battle.

I think you realise when you become a senior partner that all it really means is that you are getting older, a feeling that is reinforced on a dark, cheerless December day. You are at the age when although, God willing, you still have a good few years of practice ahead, you are already starting to suggest to people that they appoint younger partners as executors of their wills.

This was brought home to me rather forcibly the other day, when a senior partner in a firm of solicitors up the dale – admittedly some years older than myself – recounted a recent experience of his, when an executor had called at his office and greeted him in a manner which was hardly encouraging.

'Are you still here? Well, I'll be damned, I thought you'd be dead by now.'

As I remembered these words, my mood of melancholy suddenly lifted and I smiled for the first time that day. I do not believe most of us could survive for very long without a sense of humour.

There has hardly been a week this year during which I have not been consulted about a neighbour dispute. The most common causes of such arguments are boundary walls and fences, shared drives, rights of way, parking arrangements, leaking gutters and fallpipes and, in the case of agricultural properties, water rights and septic tanks.

In as many cases, however, it is the people themselves rather than the properties who are largely responsible for all the arguments. They quarrel about each others general attitude and lifestyle, about the behaviour of one another's pets, but above all they complain about noise.

I have acted for several people who have been disturbed by the musical activities of their neighbours. I still smile to myself when I remember the case of the couple who, driven mad by their neighbour's constant playing of an electric organ day and night, enlisted their entire family to form an impromptu band which produced an unholy cacophony of sound in response.

Noisy music can be a nuisance in one's own home, never mind at the neighbours, as most parents of teenage children will surely testify. For some reason which I personally cannot fathom, music to them is not music unless it is played at all times and at full volume!

Apart from noise, I have found over the years that perhaps the greatest cause of neighbour disputes is the matter of overhanging trees. I have often been asked by people what they can do if branches of a tree rooted in their neighbour's garden overhang their property. The best answer, as in all such matters, is that the problem should be rationally discussed and amicably resolved.

There are remedies in law to cover most neighbour disputes, but it should always be remembered that, after all the lawyers' letters and court cases, the people still have to live next door to each other. In extreme cases a solicitor might be tempted to advise they move move home. It could be cheaper in the long run!

In the case of overhanging trees, you can always employ self-help by cutting off the offending branches, as long as you keep strictly to your side of the boundary, but it is of course preferable that this should be done after first giving your neighbour fair warning of your intentions. Even when there has been such discussion, things can still go badly wrong, as a couple who came in to see me at the beginning of the month graphically recounted.

Stephen and Jenny have lived for many years on the outskirts of Denley in a pleasant detached house with a large garden at the back. They told me that they had always got on reasonably well with their neighbours Alec and Marlene, until the day came when they encountered the phenomenon of 'spontaneous combustion'.

The case, unique in my experience, arose in this way. Alec had approached Stephen and asked if he would mind if he cut down some of the branches on Stephen's trees which were overhanging his garden and blocking out the sunlight. In the interests of good neighbourly relations, Stephen told him he had no objection.

A few weeks later, Stephen and Jenny arrived home one afternoon after visiting some friends, and noticed to their surprise when they looked out of their lounge window that there was smoke coming from the bottom of their garden.

'I didn't know you lit a bonfire before we went out', said Jenny to her husband.

'I didn't', replied Stephen.

'Well, why is there smoke coming from the bottom of the garden?', asked Jenny.

Stephen thought for a minute and scratched his head.

'It must be a case of spontaneous combustion', he replied. 'I've read somewhere about such cases happening.'

When Stephen went down the garden to investigate, he found to his amazement a man he had never seen in his life before standing over a bonfire. He was equally surprised to see that this total stranger was being directed and supervised by Alec, who was leaning over the fence. Stephen then noticed to his dismay that, not only had the branches of his trees been chopped off, but the trees themselves had been cut right down to their roots, and the whole lot burnt on a bonfire in his own garden!

'I was speechless, Mr Francis', said Stephen after telling me the story. 'Talk about give a man an inch and he'll take a mile. What can I do about it?'

'Well', I replied, 'I'm sure we should be able to recover some damages, but the cost of replacing the trees is not likely to compensate you properly for the loss you feel. And if we have to go to court, the prospects of good neighbourly relations will be practically nil.'

'Have you had any interesting cases at the office today?', Rosemary asked me later when I returned home.

'As a matter of fact I have', I replied. 'I advised on a case of spontaneous combustion.'

Rosemary looked puzzled by this mysterious phrase, but she knew better than to press me further, for a solicitor's work is strictly confidential and can never be disclosed to anyone, not even to one's wife.

I always try to cheer up people who have been charged with motoring offences by telling them that if they have gone for five years – and many of them have gone a lot longer that that – without getting so much as a parking ticket, then they have done very well.

Many road traffic offences are very minor, and do not result in much damage to people or property, but as a motorist myself I have often been struck by the fact that aggression and violence are never very far away on the roads.

Men and women can be violent in their own homes, of course, never mind in their cars. I well remember someone once telling me that the last straw in his marriage was when 'the wife threw the goldfish bowl at me'.

When it comes to driving, however, it seems to be principally men, who, although very often meek and mild-mannered as can be outside their cars, suddenly become aggressive, threatening and violent the minute they are behind a steering wheel.

I once witnessed an amazing scene on a narrow, single track road high up on the moors, when two farmers met going in opposite directions. Neither would give way or back up to the nearest passing place. Both switched off their engines, got out of their cars and, following a preliminary stand-off in which they insulted each other in the crudest terms imaginable, they came to blows – with the result that they both required hospital treatment. They later found themselves bound over to keep the peace by the local magistrates.

I learnt not to be impatient as a motorist some years ago. I had an appointment out of the office for which I was late, through being detained by a lengthy telephone call. I ran to the car park, started my car and made for the exit. There was an old van immediately in front of me whose driver was also making for the exit, but at a snail's pace. In my impatience and frustration, I sounded my horn loudly and kept my hand firmly upon it.

The driver of the van stopped dead in his tracks, turned off his engine, got out and came towards me. I bitterly regretted my action the minute I saw the giant of a man who was fast approaching me. The expression on his face was angry – very angry.

'Na then, what's all this hootin' and tootin'?', he asked in a distinctly menacing tone of voice.

I summed up my situation and rapidly concluded that a tactful retreat was in order. As I cringed away from the window, I tried rather unconvincingly to persuade him that I had touched the horn by mistake and it had then become stuck. On the whole, I was considerably relieved to get out of that car park unscathed. My encounter with 'the big man' had taught me a lesson for life.

Curiously and coincidentally, I witnessed a very similar incident in the very same car park only the other day, but one which had an altogether more edifying result.

A motorist had found himself blocked in by another car which had been badly parked. He had obviously waited for some considerable time, and when eventually the owner of the offending car arrived he played merry hell with him. The latter may have been ignorant and inconsiderate in his choice of parking position, but after listening patiently to the tirade directed against him he said quietly:

'Nay, mister, thee an' me may both 'appen be dead afore we've gitten home for us tea.'

The offended motorist, completely taken aback by this response, was silent for a minute before he burst out laughing, shook the other warmly by the hand and said:

'You're absolutely right, my friend, life's too short for us to fall out.'

Wisdom, true wisdom, I reflected afterwards, is by no means confined to philosophers and scholars.

'Smile at us, pay us, pass us; but do not quite forget
For we are the people of England, that never have spoken yet.'

I always think of Chesterton's immortal lines from *The Secret People* whenever the subject of public footpaths crops up, for in my experience there are few topics which can stir the passions of normally tolerant Englishmen living in placid Dales communities to the same extent.

Any 'off-cumed un', however wealthy and influential he may be, who is foolish enough to attempt to deny village people their access to a footpath established by local tradition, is not likely to last very long.

Solicitors, whatever their personal views and prejudices may be, cannot pick and choose their clients. They act for both husbands and wives, landlords and tenants, employers and workers and, in the context of footpaths, they are liable to find themselves on both sides of the argument from time to time.

Earlier in the year, I successfully represented villagers in a Dales community who were objecting to an application by a local land-owner to stop up a public footpath; and yesterday, I was asked by a farmer to represent him in an application to divert a footpath which was making it awkward to farm two of his fields.

My advice in such cases is generally to 'car quiet' unless the nuisance is very great, for it is not only extremely difficult in practice to obtain a diversion order – let alone a stopping-up order – but the publicity arising from such an application is almost certain to result in more people walking there.

There is not usually any difficulty between long-established land-owners and villagers, for theirs tends to be a relationship founded upon mutual respect and co-operation, but it is a different matter when 'townies' seek to assert their perceived rights, often in an ignorant and aggressive manner.

There is likely to be continued conflict in the countryside between farmers and landowners, who have property and livestock to protect, and certain groups of ramblers who believe they have a God-given right to walk where they please.

At present, I see little evidence of any meeting of minds. Ramblers believe farmers are unnecessarily obstructive, but if this attitude does exist, then it may arise at least in part from so often finding their walls broken down and land strewn with litter. A failure to close gates can, for instance, lead to sheep, which a farmer has spent hours separating, being mixed up again in a matter of minutes.

I see the argument from both sides. When I look at the damage caused by a careless and inconsiderate minority of walkers, I sympathise with the farmers, yet I myself like to roam unfettered in the countryside. The answer, I am sure, lies in mutual tolerance and understanding, in negotiation rather than confrontation. In the meantime, however, footpaths will continue to be a touchy subject in our countryside.

I had taken a great interest in the progress of young David and Susan Taylor ever since the day just under a year ago when, with a bank loan and some financial help from their family, they started a small garden nursery on the outskirts of Denley.

They had decided that theirs was not going to be a conventional nursery or garden centre – instead they concentrated on two specialist lines. The first was contained in a series of hothouses, where they grew bananas, nectarines, and various exotic fruits and flowers which one would hardly expect to find in the Yorkshire Dales. The second was the cultivation for sale of wild flower seeds and plants. Those varieties which they did not grow themselves, they bought in from other growers.

They called in at my office last week, and I could tell by the worried expression on their faces that something was wrong. The reason for their anxiety had, they told me, arisen in the spring. They had tried to resolve it themselves during the summer and autumn, but had failed.

They had ordered from a supplier a quantity of *Centranthus* commonly known as red valerian, that delightful plant which grows in great profusion in some parts of the country, particularly on limestone cliffs. The order was for one of David and Susan's customers who wanted to try it in his garden, situated in the limestone district of upper Wharfedale.

Their supplier had in turn obtained the valerian from another grower, but when David and Susan took delivery they found to their dismay that, instead of the plants being the true wild red valerian, they were in fact the deeper coloured garden variety known as *C Coccineus*. The two suppliers had rather surprisingly thought that the two latin names were alternatives for the same plant.

David and Susan immediately realised the mistake which had been made and tried to cancel the contract, but without success. Subsequent negotiations failed, and the suppliers were threatening to sue. In desperation, David and Susan came to me for advice.

'Surely we can cancel the contract, Mr Francis', said David. 'We didn't get what we ordered.'

I think you can avoid the contract', I replied, 'but how important is your relationship with your supplier?'

'It's very important', said Susan, 'we do a lot of business with him. But surely if we can avoid the contract, so can he. After all, it was his supplier who made the mistake.'

'I don't believe so', I replied to their obvious surprise.

As David and Susan had been outlining their problem I had remembered from my law student days the rather quirky facts in *Rose v Pim*, perhaps the classic case of 'mistake in contract'.

The case was about a contract for the sale of a type of horse bean called féveroles, arranged through a middle-man. The latter delivered to the supplier a quantity of Moroccan horse beans, which they both believed to be the same as féveroles. The buyer knew better and refused to accept them.

The question for the court was whether the supplier had any remedy against the middle-man. Its decision was that he had not, because although they had both mistakenly thought that féveroles and Moroccan horse beans were the same, the contract could not be avoided, as there had been clear outward agreement and the subject matter of the contract actually existed.

How important it is in life, I have always thought since first learning that case, that you should be able to tell the difference between féveroles and Moroccan horse beans, and to know that féveroles are not just any old horse beans but are a very special medium-sized variety of horse bean!

After I had finished telling them all about this rather complicated case, David looked at Susan and smiled for the first time.

'Well, we've learnt something today. I'd never heard of féveroles before. So what's your advice, Mr Francis?'

'It all depends on whether you think the game's worth the candle', I replied. 'Do you want to stick to your legal rights and perhaps lose a valuable relationship with your supplier, or would it be better to consider settling the bill and putting it down to experience?'

'I think we'd better have a think about it and let you know', said David.

I suddenly had another thought as they left the office.

'If you do decide to accept the garden valerian after all, let me know because I could do with half a dozen plants for one of my borders. They are marvellous for attracting peacocks and red admirals in late autumn.'

'Right, Mr Francis, we'll bear that in mind', said David with a grin, as he and his wife went out through the door and into the busy street outside.

Rosemary and I went Christmas shopping last weekend, and spent most of our time in a large toy shop where we looked for presents to give to the children of relations and friends.

As we walked around the shop and I contemplated the vast array of computer games, pocket electronics, space and science fiction games, and just about every conceivable type of modern technological gadgetry which money can buy, I could not help wondering where all the toys of my own childhood had gone, particularly those memorable toys which featured in all our family Christmases.

Where, for instance, were blow football, and that delightfully simple cricket game Howzat? Where were the 'flick cards', which we held firmly in the hand and flicked rapidly one after the other to produce a moving picture sequence? Where, too, were those memorable little toy sweet shops with their miniature jars of goodies, tiny scales to weigh them on and cardboard money with which to purchase them? Where were all those kaleidoscopes which made incredibly fascinating patterns from pieces of coloured paper when shaken? Where were light-up bow ties, seebackroscopes, button holes which squirted water, Davy Crocket hats and joke perfume boxes with jump-out rats? Where were stilts, pogo sticks, clay marbles, hula-hoops, skipping ropes, yo-yos and spud guns?

I found, on looking further around the shop, that only a few of these favourites had survived, along with those two splendid board games Monopoly and Cluedo, which we played for hours on rainy days when we grew tired of Winalot, Contraband, Ludo, Whist, Rummy, Snap, Happy Families and Pelmanism.

The best Christmas presents I ever received were a bicycle, a leather football, a butterfly net and fishing rod, though not necessarily in that order. One year Santa Claus struggled to carry a Punch and Judy stand into my bedroom, and another year he left me a buddleia bush, which I planted on Christmas day and which for years afterwards attracted masses of red admirals, peacocks and small tortoiseshells when it flowered every August. Not many of my presents lasted that long.

One year my sister received a cooking set. She made some delicious peppermint creams and I proudly produced a tray of toffee biscuits. I thought they were brilliant, an opinion sadly not shared by the rest of of the family, who spent the day picking their teeth and made me solemnly promise never to offer them again!

My nostalgic reminiscences were suddenly interrupted by a tap on the shoulder from Rosemary.

'Well, have you had a good look?', she asked. 'Have you any suggestions?'

I hesitated, not wanting to let on that I had not been applying my mind to the subject in hand.

'I'm not sure', I replied lamely. 'What do you think we should buy?'

As we left the shop, I was still seeing in my mind's eye the toys and games of my childhood, and I felt sad in a way to think that many of them have seemingly gone for ever. The children of today naturally know only the more sophisticated toys and technological wonders of the late twentieth century, and there is no rational reason why parents should expect them to appreciate the music, toys or books loved by an earlier generation. The past, as they say, is another country.

Rosemary and I eventually completed our shopping, and Christmas has come and gone. We spent it, as we always do, at home with the family, all together, children and grown-ups and this year spread over four generations.

We went to church to remind ourselves of the true meaning of Christmas, and to sing all the old favourite carols. I was glad that we did, for I echo the thoughts of Hilaire Belloc when he wrote:

'I pray good beef and I pray good beer
This holiest night of all the year.
But I pray detestable drink for them
That give no honour to Bethlehem.'

Christmas is still for me a marvellous and magical time; exchanging cards, giving and receiving presents, decorating the tree (and praying that the fairy lights stay lit), re-enacting the wondrous legend of Santa Claus, listening for the sound of reindeer and filling stockings at the end of the bed, pulling crackers and playing silly games, watching the *Wizard of Oz* on television, escaping the dull routine of work and just for a time shutting out the whole incomprehensible world.

As we sat down to Christmas lunch, I kept assuring Rosemary that the turkey, as always, had been cooked to perfection and none of the trimmings had been forgotten. I managed to find a few old silver threepenny bits to hide in the Christmas pudding, and we toasted each other with glasses filled with champagne, a drink which is all the more pleasurable for being affordable but once a year.

After lunch, my daughter Melanie played the piano and we all sang some carols. Johnny, whose voice has not yet broken and who sings beautifully in a clear treble voice, and I, whose musical talents are strangely unrecognised, sang *Good King Wenceslas*, taking the parts of page and monarch respectively.

As I played my part in this duet, I smiled to myself at the realisation that I, an Englishman, still slightly merry from the effects of the champagne, should be impersonating a king of Bohemia who is said to have 'neglected business for pleasure and been much addicted to drunkenness'.

Christmas is above all, I think, a season for remembering happy family times past, and re-living your own childhood Christmases through the excited faces of today's children.

It is all very sentimental and nostalgic, of course, but there should surely be no criticism on that score, for they are feelings which come from the heart, and somehow eternally shine through the blatant materialism and crude commercialism of the modern Christmas.

On New Year's Eve we were sitting alone again by the fireside. Our young people (for we must learn not to call them children any more) had left everything and all gone out to their different parties.

'It looks as though it will have to be the old firm again', I said to Rosemary, as we went through to the kitchen to tackle the washing up.

Afterwards, back in the lounge I put another log on the fire. As we relaxed in our armchairs, we talked together, as parents do, of how much our children had grown up during the year, of the ups and downs we had shared, and of the changes, joys and sorrows which had arisen in the wider circle of family and friends.

We recalled our holidays on Mull and in Devon, and talked of special days and events which lingered in our minds.

We went on to exchange our own favourite memories of the year in the countryside, the garden and our dales community. Mine of the cricket at Denley Show; hers of the day the first swallows arrived and of flocks of fieldfares in late autumn. Mine of bilberrying on the heather moors; hers of watching our pet lambs frolicking in the field and lying down contentedly with our puppy. Mine of seeing a field of harebells alight with common blues, so that I could scarcely tell flowers and butterflies apart; hers of the rockery in full bloom. Mine of planting potatoes on Good Friday in accordance with the Dales tradition, cropping them in late summer and feeling secure for the winter; hers of finding a wren's nest. Mine of the fragrant scent of honeysuckle, lavender and roses on a July evening; hers of the friendship and community spirit at the annual church bazaar. And so we went on, until after a while we fell silent, intuitively leaving each other to our own thoughts.

Mine turned automatically to the year past at work. I recalled cases won and lost, files of which I was proud – and others I would rather forget. I remembered too how often I had felt my workload was too great, that I was like a juggler with too many balls in the air at the same time, and how I kept having to remind myself of Browning's line that 'a man's reach should extend his grasp or what's a heaven for?'

What, I wondered, did all those conveyances, leases, wills, divorces, probates, court cases, partnership agreements and all the other legal work I had done really amount to, and was it all worthwhile? An old Yorkshire solicitor once said to me:

'All we do, lad, is to sweep the road a bit cleaner.'

Perhaps that is the best that can truly be said.

There would for certain be more conveyances, wills and probates next year, along with all the other amazingly varied cases which a country solicitor has to tackle, but it would, as always, be the clients who would make the practice of the law both interesting and worthwhile.

Would 'Lucky Jim', I wondered , be in to see me with further tales of woe? Would brothers Joe and Fred Westgate still be playing their famous double act to thwart advisers and officials alike? Would my good friends George and Elinor Dixon still be joking about sending a crate of whisky to their alcoholic cousin Joseph to hasten his demise and thereby inherit a trust fund? Would farmer Fred Hellifield still be bossing his 'missus' around and boasting that, in his neck of the woods, 'men were still men and women glad of 'em'? Would 'ockard old bugger' Jack Higgins remain a client of mine, and if so would I ever be able to complete a job to his satisfaction? Would Muriel Smith recover from her court appearance on a shoplifting charge and still bravely say 'good morning' to the world? Would George and Albert Wright still talk to me interminably about sheep and bees, instead of the legal business in hand, and would old Mr Noble still measure his work by 'reckovee'?

The firelight flickered as my thoughts turned from clients, characters and cases to life in general at the latter end of the twentieth century.

A solicitor is, I suppose, a prime witness of the human condition. He sees joy and sorrow, victory and defeat, relief and despair, black and white and every shade of grey.

We live in an increasingly violent and materialistic world in which there is cruelty and injustice, sadness, misery and suffering. Yet at

166

the same time there is still kindness and courage, labour, laughter and love, the abiding and incorruptible fruits of the human spirit. In a frenetic age, the English countryside is there for all who are wise and innocent enough to enjoy it, and the eternal verities still stand for all of sufficient faith.

My reflections were suddenly interrupted by a knock on the back door, which I got up to answer. When I returned to the lounge, I found that Rosemary had spread a pattern on the floor and was starting to cut out a dress – and this after all her prodigious feats of cooking, entertaining and coping with all the varied demands of the family over Christmas. Truly a woman's work is never done.

'Come on', I said, 'we've been invited to drinks across the road. Let's go and see the old year out and wish luck to the new.'